The Joy Of NOT Being Married

Married

The Essential Guide For Singles
(And Those Who Wish They Were)

Ernie J. Zelinski

VIP BOOKS

Distributed to US Bookstores by:
Login Publishers Consortium

Chicago, Illinois

VIP BOOKS Edition

Published by:
Visions International Publishing
Edmonton, Alberta, Canada

Distributed to U.S. bookstores by:
Login Publishers Consortium, Chicago, Illinois
Telephone (312) 733-8228, Fax (312) 733-3107

95 96 97 98 99 PS/RRD 10 9 8 7 6 5 4 3 2 1

Cover design and illustrations by Vern Busby

Direct any inquiries to:

Ernie J. Zelinski, c/o Visions International Publishing
Box 4072, Edmonton, Alberta, Canada, T6E 4S8

Publisher's Cataloging in Publication
(Prepared by Quality Books Inc.)

Zelinski, Ernie J.
    The joy of not being married : (the essential guide for singles
and those who wish they were) / Ernie J. Zelinski.
    p. cm.
    Includes bibliographical references.
    ISBN 0-9694194-3-0

    1. Single people--Life skills guides.   I. Title.

HQ800.Z45 1995   305.9'0652

                                    QB195-20034

.... to all the creative and well-balanced singles in this world, who have thought about that special someone they still haven't met, and refuse to settle for a dull compromise.

Acknowledgments

My thanks go out to the following team of kind individuals who were adventurous enough to read the manuscript and offer their advice. The many comments and opinions were invaluable in helping me complete this challenging project.

Forrest Bard
Peter Borchers
Joy Harrish
Evelyn Lang
Ross Bradford
Wyatt Cavanaugh
Linda Shaben
Harvey Deutschendorf
Henry Dammeyer
Roger Kent
Dan O'Brien
Diana Samoaa
Jim MacKenzie
Dale Young
Henry Dembicki
Liz Sherman
Anne Nachi

Special Acknowledgment

A special thank you to Ben Kerr for allowing me to use the words to his two songs, *"The Joy Of Not Working Nine To Five"* And *"The Joy Of Not Being Married,"* in this book.

Table Of Contents

Important - Disclaimer

The purpose of this book is to inform, educate, challenge, and entertain the reader. The book's content is not meant to be a substitute for any professional services.

This book is sold with the understanding that neither the author nor the publisher is engaged in rendering legal, psychological, medical, or any other profession advice. If such advice or other assistance is required, the personal services of competent professionals should be found.

Any decisions made by the reader as a result of reading this book are made at the sole responsibility of the reader. The author and publisher assume no liability for any such decisions.

Preface

This book is for you if you are single and looking for something more to enhance your life. My objective is to show all singles the many opportunities to enjoy life without a relationship. Regardless of your age, sex, financial status, and marital history, you can embrace single life and make it a satisfying experience. Today, singlehood offers a rich mixture of options, identities, and lifestyles. It isn't always easy being a single in a couples-crazed world; society looks suspiciously at singles - especially happy ones. However, being happy being single is easier than most people think. *"The Joy Of Not Being Married"* is about how to live life to the fullest. If you are single, this is the time to be all that you can be.

Whether by choice or by chance, more people than ever before are now remaining single. Marriage is less significant to North Americans. There are more singles today than ever before, in numbers, and as a percentage of the population. Due to divorce, later marriages, and choosing to remain unattached, more of us are spending major parts of our adult lives being single.

> *"Marriage is like a besieged fortress. Everyone outside wants to get in, and everyone inside wants to get out."*
>
> *- Quitard*

Somewhere along the way, most of us have been indoctrinated with the notion of the ideal marriage that we all deserve. However, many of us are finding the story-book marriage difficult, or impossible, to create. Many singles are still locked into that dream, regardless of how unrealistic the dream may appear at times. Many people feel cheated because they haven't attained their dream marriage. Some singles still hope for the fairy-tale marriage; others have given up all hope and resigned themselves to a life of despair.

The main focus of this book isn't on how to create that special relationship or dream marriage. The intention of this book is to help you make the best out of being single. If you still aspire to having a long-term intimate relationship, that's okay. You will certainly stand a much greater chance of attaining it being happy in your present situation, than being unhappy and desperate for it. Alternatively, if you have shopped around for the ideal marriage, and concluded that it isn't likely to happen, then you must make singlehood worth living to get satisfaction out of life.

To some readers, the title of this book may imply that I feel there is something wrong with marrage. I want to emphasize that I am not trying to undermine the institution of marriage. The foundation of this book is that if people aren't married, they can make being single a happy experience. To warn you in advance, I make no attempt to be politically correct. I also make no attempt to cater to intellectuals. In my books, I avoid great detail, unending facts, and academic jargon, which only distract most sensible readers from what they really want to read.

> *"Intellectuals should never marry; they won't enjoy it; and besides, they should not reproduce themselves."*
>
> *- Don Herold*

The essence of this book is how to enhance your purpose in life, how to create a better sense of community, and how to celebrate being alone. I have discovered certain character traits are important for singles to be happy and live life to the fullest. The common thread among successful and inspirational singles is they have an important purpose in life. They also have a strong sense of community, established through a number of close, meaningful relationships. Although these relationships aren't as intimate as typical marital relationships, the relationships are still very important for support and companionship. Inspirational singles also have high self-esteem. Because they like themselves, successful singles know how to enjoy themselves when they are alone.

As you read the rest of this book, remember that there isn't one magical formula for being a happy single individual. Because some parts of this book may not apply to your present situation, you may want to utilize some parts, and disregard the rest. You get to take responsibility for what to apply to your life. What you apply will depend on your interests, goals, and direction in life. Exciting lifestyles for singles have emerged which would have been frowned upon not that long ago. Today, regardless of your sex, age, or past marital status, you can create a happy and fulfilling lifestyle that will defy explanation to many single and married individuals.

1. Married To The Single Life?

I would be married, but I'd have no wife.

I would be married to the single life.

- Richard Crashaw (Poet in 17th Century)

The Easy Way To Being Happy Being Single

I have written this book to celebrate single life by showing the many pleasures and opportunities it has to offer. Being single has given me the opportunity to create a career that I truly love, and develop friendships that I may not have had the opportunity to develop, if I was married. Singlehood has also given me the luxury of freedom and independence to pursue a wide range of leisure experiences that most married people don't have the opportunity to experience.

For purposes of this book, I am not drawing only on my own experiences. There are many ways that single people attain happiness. The greater part of this book is the result of studying and listening to the stories, experiences, and aspirations of other singles. Many singles have zest, energy, and joie de vivre which surprises many married people. The important point is that well-balanced, happy singles enjoy being single. To them, life is more than just something to do while waiting for someone special to show up.

"I think, therefore I am single."

- Liz Winston

"I never knew what true happiness was until I got married. Now it's too late."

High-flying singles know that life is not always easy; they realize that they have to do some difficult things to attain satisfaction in life. If you have read either of my two previous books, then you know about The Easy Rule Of Life. This rule states that when we continually choose to do the easy and comfortable things, life ends up being difficult. However, when we do the difficult and uncomfortable things, life often ends up being easy. The Easy Rule Of Life influences every area of single life including work, financial gain, friendship, love, health, leisure, and overall satisfaction. (For a more detailed explanation of The Easy Rule Of Life, see the Appendix on page 170.)

Ashleigh Brilliant said: "I have abandoned the search for truth, and am now looking for a good fantasy." I trust that you haven't done the same. It is important that you aren't carried away by illusions about singlehood. The bad news is that this book can't lead you to that Promised Land, about halfway between Nirvana and Shangri-la. If you were expecting that single life could be one big party, I am sorry to have disappointed you.

After the bad news, I have some really good news. The good news is that all single individuals - including you - can live in a singles paradise. To have a happy and successful life, you must utilize the Easy Rule Of Life and follow the principles in this book.

Well-balanced singles know that The Easy Rule Of Life applies to any area of life from which we can achieve satisfaction. For example, while writing this book during the summer of 1995, I had to confront the difficult and uncomfortable. Since my philosophy is that I should avoid working in any month that doesn't have an "r" in it, I had other plans to spend the summer taking it easy in Vancouver. Furthermore, the idea for this book started as a joke when I responded to a challenging and humorous comment made by my friend Forrest. Even when I mentioned my idea for this book to my American and Canadian distributors, I wasn't serious about writing it. However, having confronted the difficult and uncomfortable by undertaking this challenging project, I am seeing that my life is already easier due to the satisfaction I have already experienced.

Being happy as a single is dependent upon making up your mind to make the best of your situation. This will take some effort; it will also be uncomfortable at times. Taking the easy and comfortable way - sitting at home and blaming the world - will put you on a dead-end street. Long-term satisfaction can only be attained by undertaking the challenging activities which are at times somewhat difficult. A price has to paid in terms of time and effort. If you are no longer a juvenile, you should have learned by now that nothing of major consequence in life comes easily. You must pay the price of a little discomfort for anything that adds to your long-term happiness.

You may now be thinking the same thing that a woman at a recent seminar said to me: "Ernie Zelinski, who are you? Some kind of sadist? You are advocating nothing but a whole lot of suffering in this world for me." On the contrary, I am not advocating anything of that nature. Keep in mind that I don't work more than four or five hours a day. Also, as much as possible, I avoid working in any month that doesn't have an "r" in it. This is not suffering. I enjoy life - it is more than just something to do. I am a proponent of a little discomfort now and then, which all adds up to a big payoff of satisfaction and happiness in the long term.

> *"If you want the rainbow, you gotta put up with the rain."*
>
> *- Dolly Parton*

Have you ever experienced an incredible high after you accomplished something that you initially didn't think you could, or something that everyone else said couldn't be done? For example, if you quit smoking, I bet what you accomplished wasn't easy. And yet, by undertaking the difficult and uncomfortable, you achieved a great deal of satisfaction from your accomplishment. This was The Easy Rule Of Life in action.

Being happy being single takes commitment and effort. You must take responsibility for your life if you want to create a singles paradise where you are happy and fulfilled. You have already taken some responsibility by starting to read this book. Richard Bach in his book "*Illusions*" wrote: "Every person, all the events of your life are there because you have drawn them there." Let's say that at some level you took responsibility and utilized your tremendous mental powers to create me writing this book for you. Yes, if it wasn't for you, in the summer of 1995 I could have been cycling around Stanley Park, wining and dining at the English Bay Cafe, and having coffee at the Bread Garden and Starbucks, while waiting for my soulmate to show up. However, I trust that you will allow me to take at least the next two summers off, so I can do these, and a host of other enjoyable things, before you use your mental powers to create me writing another book for you.

Knowing Where The Scissors Are - Your Singles Advantage

Voluntary singles enjoy their position in life. They realize that marriage isn't essential for happiness. Singlehood gives carefree individuals the luxury of getting much more in touch with themselves. They have made singlehood a lifestyle choice. At one time, they may have been married to someone; now, they are married to the single life.

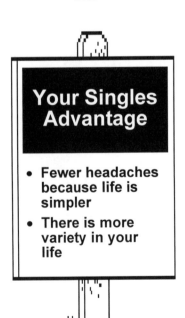

Your Singles Advantage

- **Fewer headaches because life is simpler**
- **There is more variety in your life**

Why do voluntary singles choose single life over married life? Obviously, there have to be some advantages of singlehood. One day, I asked my friend Dan if he had recently met any women he was interested in dating, or even marrying. Dan, married on two previous occasions, replied: "I'm not interested now. What I really like about not being married is I always know where the scissors are."

Knowing where the scissors are is a pretty powerful reason for being single. Who needs more? Of course, there are many other advantages of singlehood in North American society. Some of the many advantages are scattered throughout this book in the "Your Singles Advantage" signs like the one on the left. I have done this to

6

keep reminding you of the many opportunities for enjoying the pleasures of single life.

If You Are Single, You Are Not Alone

It is easy for a single in a crowd of married individuals to fall into the trap of thinking that everyone else is out there with someone special. If you are single and feel alone, think again. More North Americans are single than ever before, and the numbers keep steadily going up. There is a burgeoning culture of single life out there. Today, the singles lifestyle is okay; there is far less stigma associated with being single than there was in the past. A person can be forty years old and single without having to justify this to every new person. Many happy singles are well-educated, healthy, highly intelligent, and very successful in their careers.

> *"My boyfriend and I broke up. He wanted to get married and I didn't want him to."*
>
> Rita Rudner

On the West Coast, in places like Seattle and San Francisco, flying solo is even trendy. In the Vancouver electoral district held by former Canadian Prime Minister Kim Campbell, 65 percent of adults are single and 55 percent are singles living alone. There are actually individuals who had been happily married when they decided to give up their marriages to be on their own. This may seem ridiculous to some people, but these individuals now report they are glad that they opted for singlehood.

Why would anyone choose to be single when a happy marriage is available? The solo life offers contentment for these formerly married singles, as it does for many never-married singles. Many happy singles don't necessarily rule out an intimate relationship in the future, but for now, they are happy to fly solo. The freedom and flexibility of singlehood gives them a lifestyle which offers more variety than marriage. Let's look at some of the reasons why the number of singles in North America keeps increasing.

> *"Marriage is ridiculous"*
>
> - Goldie Hawn

Many singles don't want to get into a relationship and miss out on the many activities that single life has to offer. A relationship

> *"It's a funny thing that when a man hasn't anything on earth to worry about, he goes off and gets married."*
>
> *- Robert Frost*

takes time, energy, and money. Time is precious, energy is limited, and sufficient money can be hard to come by. With the flexibility they have, singles can date and expand their social network. They can also indulge in a wide range of leisure activities, from joining a fitness club to going on a cruise alone. Singles can more readily pursue career and travel opportunities, because their time, energy, and money aren't tied up in a relationship.

To truly happy singles, being unattached is the optimal situation for the time being, but not necessarily for the future. Happy voluntary singles aren't single because they can't find a marriage partner. Social experts state that happy voluntary singles, unlike many single and married people, have a true sense of themselves and can be happy with - or without - a relationship.

Some happy unattached individuals are professional singles who have an unending number of friendships and romantic experiences with members of the opposite sex. They have no desire to change their situation to anything resembling marriage. Freedom, independence, and variety are overwhelming positives of single life.

Not all voluntary singles are operating out of the overwhelming positives of singlehood. Some singles are terrified of long-term relationships. Two phobias may interfere with their success at creating relationships. The first is amorphobia which is the fear of intimacy in relationships. Romantic success frightens some singles because they are afraid of having to reveal themselves to others. The second phobia is gamophobia which is the fear of marriage. Gamophobia describes the excessive fear of commitment and all the other adjustments that marriage demands. If gamophobics were to find Mr. or Ms. Right, they would still be afraid of marriage. They fear being dependent on someone, or having someone dependent on them. With so many marriages breaking up around them, they may also fear being abandoned by a marriage partner, or having to abandon a partner.

> *"Never get married while you're going to college; it's hard to get a start if a prospective employer finds you've already made one mistake."*
>
> *- Kin Hubbard*

Other voluntary singles aren't necessarily as happy as they would like to be, but they are fairly happy being single. For example, my friend Bob is certain he never wants to get married. He says that he prefers living alone because of the hassles that arise while living with another person. He is convinced that he can't stand living with someone else, and is committed to living alone for the rest of his life. It isn't that Bob doesn't like women; he adores them. However, he just is not prepared to tolerate the inconveniences of living with someone.

> *"Marriage is a great institution, but I'm not ready for an institution."*
>
> *- Mae West*

Divorce and separation, which are much more prevalent than they were in your and my Grandmothers' time, have increased the number of singles. In 1993, 2.3 million couples got married in the U.S., but at the same time 1.6 million couples officially agreed their marriages couldn't be saved. In Canada, four out of ten marriages end in divorce.

The number of singles has increased due to changes in the workplace. Social experts point out that, with more women working at higher paying jobs, marriage is no longer as necessary for women's economic survival as it once was. Many women also won't marry unless they can marry "up," that is, marry someone with a higher income than they make. This self-imposed constraint reduces their chances of getting married.

Sociologists have attributed the large number of singles to a variety of reasons. Statistics indicate that singles in North America constitute a large minority. By choice, or due to circumstances beyond their control, more people than ever before are remaining single. Some singles are divorced, some are separated, some are widowed, and others have never been attached. According to a recent survey, there are 25,000,000 people in North America who are unattached and living by themselves. As the above numbers indicate, if you are single, you aren't alone.

So, What Do You Really Want?

Voluntary and truly happy singles are self-confident and know what is really important to them. They don't want the complications of marriage at this time; instead, they will settle for the simplicity of single life. Single life is a situation they enjoy. At this time, they don't desire the drastically different situation that marriage would create. Presently, they are married to the single life.

> *"My wife and I were happy for twenty years. Then we met."*
>
> *- Rodney Dangerfield*

In life, there is no substitute for happiness. Knowing what we want out of life is a large part of the battle in being happy. The problem is that many single people haven't stopped to clearly define what they want. Happy, high-flying singles know all the things that they want, and how to take action in order to get them.

The first indispensable step in leading a satisfying life is taking the time to determine what you truly want. So, what do you want? Sure, you want to look better, feel better, work less, make huge amounts of money, have more leisure time, and become more important. I know that! Doesn't everyone want these things? All humans want to be comfortable with the least amount of effort. The problem is these things won't bring you any satisfaction and happiness if you don't put in some effort into creating them. If everything in life was easy, you would appreciate nothing.

You must be able to answer some simple sounding questions, but ones which aren't easy to answer. What do you want in life? Are you prepared to put in the effort required? How are you going to get what you want? It is essential that you write down what you want - everything that is important to you - from satisfying employment, to a comfortable place in which to live, to an intimate relationship. Now what do you really want in terms of making a difference in this world? This should be something that will take some effort and put you at risk. Getting what you want will require that you vacate your comfort zone. You must also show some motivation and courage.

Creating a relationship so you can get married may be one of your wants. That's okay. You must do something about this. Chapter 9 on *Tips For The Romantically Challenged* will help. The warning is that you shouldn't make this your overriding goal, and exclude other goals in your life. Many singles feel their lives must be left in limbo until Mr. or Ms. Right appears. They think that they can start planning for the future only when they have found the ideal marriage partner with whom they will live happily ever after.

> *"If you want to sacrifice the admiration of many men for the criticism of one, go ahead, get married."*
>
> *- Katharine Hepburn*

10

It is important that you don't put your life on hold until you find a relationship. You must move ahead toward your long-term goals based on the possibility that you may not find that relationship for some time. Putting your life on hold, while waiting for the relationship to appear, means you are putting off some important pursuits and activities. You are short changing yourself by limiting your happiness and satisfaction. Being single is an opportune time to exercise your freedom of mind, and to pursue worthwhile and satisfying goals for yourself.

"Kiss me and I will turn into a man, marry you, and give you everything you can expect in marriage."

"I would rather remain single and have a talking frog for a pet."

You should be prepared to adjust your goals to live with a partner if you meet Mr. Right or Ms. Right, but it is important that you be prepared to live single for the rest of your life. Neglecting your personal goals, on the assumption that the right marriage partner will come along, will have a negative impact on your happiness. You must remove the pressure of trying to find a marriage partner. If you aren't as happy as you can be being single, you are less likely to attain your goal of creating a meaningful relationship.

Ambiguous goals will get you ambiguous results. If you are tentative about what you are looking and striving for, life will become dull and dejecting. You must know how to set a goal, and what to do to get there. You should look at where you want to be a year from now, and then again five or ten years from now, so you have something you are looking forward to achieving outside a relationship. This may be difficult, but you must do it. No one else is going to decide for you. Taking action on goal setting will clarify your dreams and aspirations. At this time, your plans should be contingent on what you want to pursue in life as a happy single individual, and not contingent on what you want to pursue with someone else once you meet him or her.

Some married people regret having married and some single people regret not having married. However, well-balanced single individuals don't waste their energy regretting anything. Whether you are a voluntary or involuntary single, happiness is a choice. Since you are single, why shouldn't you get the most out of single life?

Again, being a happy single individual is highly dependent upon your achievements in the areas of leisure activities, establishing a sense of community, enjoying your time alone, and discovering your personal mission. To be happy, you must look at what you want to change in your life. If you want to be slimmer, become a better tennis player, have more money, be less overworked, and have more friends, then you have to put some effort into these areas. Achievements in these areas will make for a happier you.

While reading the rest of this book, you may find that the content in Chapter 2 and Chapter 3 challenges some of your beliefs about whether being married can greatly add to happiness and self-esteem. If you have no difficulty with these two chapters, then - with a little motivation and effort - you will be well on your way to being a well-balanced and high-flying single.

Your Singles Advantage

- **The last cold beer is always yours**
- **You don't irk a spouse when you repair your bicycle in the bathtub**

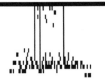

Many of the advantages of being single relate to independence and not being disturbed. Being single is about freedom - freedom to sleep late, watch a soap opera, or go visit that charming member of the opposite sex at the coffee bar. Being single also affords the time and freedom to write a book, go for a ten-mile bicycle ride, or talk to a friend for two hours, without being disturbed by a demanding spouse. More time is available to sit back and determine what you really want. If you know what you are looking for, you will be able to spot it when it presents itself. Making the most out of being single means taking advantage of the freedom to create a lifestyle that is adventurous, exciting, and rewarding for you.

2. Singlehood: The State Of Your True Self

Choosing Either A Singles Prison Or A Singles Paradise

A great mystery to me is why so many people choose to blame the world instead of taking responsibility for their lives. For singles, this is a choice between a singles prison or a singles paradise. Because you have taken the responsibility to read this book, I will assume that, if you aren't already there, you are well on your way to living in a singles paradise.

Nonetheless, I will touch on the dangers of the victim mentality. A Globe and Mail editorial recently stated that the 1990s is the decade of the victim. Since it is even trendy in some social circles to be a victim, I must take the time to warn you of the potential consequences, in case you ever come close to falling into the mental trap of unnecessarily thinking you are a victim. Many singles look at themselves as victims when, if fact, they aren't. These individuals have voluntarily put themselves in a singles prison; they look at life as a rip-off because they aren't married or coupled. These singles blame society, their parents, their country's economic state, or the world in general for their unhappiness and loneliness.

> "If your daily life seems poor, do not blame it; blame yourself, tell yourself that you are not poet enough to call forth its riches."
>
> - Rainer Maria Rilke

About ten years ago, I was driving a 55-year-old member from my tennis club to pick up his car. In our discussion, I casually mentioned that when I was a teen, I tended to blame my parents for a lot of things, but since then I realized they did the best they could with what they knew. I further mentioned that I was aware of adults over 30 years old who were still blaming their parents for most of

13

their problems. I was surprised when this man replied that he himself still blamed his parents for a lot of the troubles in his life, including his failed relationships. I thought this was a little strange for a man of 55 whose parents had been dead for years, and who had children of his own.

> *"The only prison we need to escape from is the prison of our own minds."*
>
> *- Unknown Wise Person*

Much to my further surprise, since that time ten years ago, parent bashing has become acceptable in the 1990s. It has even become a trendy pastime for many adults as manifested by the coverage on TV talk shows and psychology magazines. The parent bashers refer to themselves as "Adult Children" (a rather curious term indeed).

These Adult Children have been known to pass blame for their own current problems in adulthood, such as alcoholism, drug addiction, divorce, and incompatible relationships, unto their parents. What is wrong with this? The problem with Adult Children is their unwillingness to take responsibility for their own actions. They suffer from a victim mentality and attempt to shun responsibility for anything and everything distasteful in their lives.

To show how absurd it is for these Adult Children to blame their parents for their problems, let me go back to a seminar in which I participated a few years ago During the seminar proceedings, one of the 257 participants was confronted by the seminar leader when the participant mentioned that many of his personal problems were due to his less-than-perfect parents. To emphasize to this misguided participant how wrong he was to think that he was disadvantaged because of his parents, the seminar leader asked the rest of us 256 participants to raise our hands if we thought that we had excellent or close-to-perfect parents. Much to the surprise of this participant, not one hand went up. As the seminar leader pointed out, the 257 participants represented a wide range of backgrounds, and not one of them had even remotely perfect parents.

> *"Take your life in your own hands, and what happens? A terrible thing: no one to blame."*
>
> *- Erica Jong*

Michele Wiener-Davis, a well-known professional therapist, has shown great integrity in writing her excellent book *"Fire Your Shrink,"*

14

in which she talks about the dangers of the victim mentality, and why therapy usually doesn't work for most people who see "shrinks." Many people with the victim mentality spend countless hours fixating on their problems in the company of highly paid therapists - who are bored with their clients' stories, and spend most of their working hours contemplating whether they should buy a new Mercedes or BMW. As Michele Wiener-Davis has discovered, people with the victim mentality spend months, or even years, passing blame, and never get around to taking responsibility for actually solving their problems. Of course, therapists benefit from clients not having solved their problems, because the clients keep coming back with money in their hands to help pay for the Mercedes and BMWs.

Your Singles Advantage

- **Life is more exciting**
- **No one uses your personal effects**
- **You have more clothes-closet space**

The thing that impresses me about people with the victim mentality is how much energy they will put into shunning responsibility and complicating their lives. The idea that one is responsible for most of one's situations in life is difficult for someone with the victim mentality to accept. Here are some of the thoughts afflicting singles with the victim mentality:

- My ex-husband/ex-wife is to blame for all my problems.
- Men/women are so different from the way they should be.
- If I was married, I would be a lot happier with myself.
- Changing myself is impossible because I was born this way.
- My less-than-perfect parents are responsible for my inability to make my life work.
- Governments don't do enough for people like myself.
- I shouldn't be subjected to the discomfort of rejection.
- The world ought to be different.
- I am totally disadvantaged because I am not attractive like many people.
- Why isn't everyone as nice to me as I am to everyone?

Negative singles with the victim mentality have perverted beliefs;

> *"When you are looking for obstacles, you can't find opportunities."*
>
> *- J.C. Bell*

they attempt to transfer all blame to parents, friends, ex-spouses, strangers, society, or the government. By choosing the above thoughts, singles are victims of their own incorrect thinking. How can singles with the victim mentality escape from a singles prison and move into a singles paradise? In her book, Wiener-Davis writes about people who used to suffer from the victim mentality, and now have become winners by turning their lives around. She states: "People who live their dreams are those who stop considering all the angles, weighing the pros and cons, and just do it .... They've come to realize it's time to stop talking to their friends, families, or therapists, ... and begin living. Without action there is no change."

Winning at the singles game takes action and achievement. The ability to be a happy single person isn't something anyone is born with. All singles can lead fulfilling lives, if they take responsibility for themselves, and refrain from thinking of themselves as victims. Instead of justifying why they are victims, and ending up in a singles prison, winning singles look for opportunities, take advantage of them, and end up living in a singles paradise.

Belief Is A Disease

Jean-Paul Sartre said: "Existence is absurd." All existence may not be absurd, but certain human behavior is extremely absurd. In September, 1995, Toronto Sun writer Linda Barnard reported on single women who have engaged the services of a company called Fantasy International to organize mock weddings. These fantasy affairs can come complete with a stand-in groom, extra actors to play the bridesmaids, minister, and guests, photos, and a full dinner and reception. Fantasy doesn't come cheap in this case. One "wannabe" bride paid $6,000 to have a fake wedding arranged - the cost of her dress, flowers, food, drinks, and fees for the actors was extra. While discussing this article with my friend Joy, we both concluded that even spending $6,000 on a real wedding is ridiculous.

> *"The most dangerous cake I ever ate was wedding cake."*
>
> *- Unknown Wise Person*

The majority of the public probably feel that

women staging costly fake weddings have major problems. In the Toronto Sun article, psychiatrist Dr. Irwin Wolkoff was quoted as saying that there was potential for emotional disaster for these fantasy brides, especially for those who didn't fully understand the implications. For women who have a full understanding of what is going on, the fantasy wedding is similar in experience to men hiring a high-class prostitute according to Dr. Wolkoff. The queen-for-a-day theory discussed in Chapter 3 further explains why these women want to have the experience of a mock wedding.

> *"I've never been married, but I tell people I'm divorced so they won't think something is wrong with me."*
>
> *- Elayne Boosler*

The amount of money "wannabe" brides will pay just to experience a fake wedding shows how much emphasis certain factions of our society place on wedding ceremonies and marriage. Fantasy brides desperately wanting to experience a marriage ceremony - real or fake - have defined themselves in societal roles. They must realize that there is more to them as individuals than what society and their families want them to be. Being single doesn't mean being deprived of the good life.

The idea of being single is sometimes more challenging and aggravating than actually being single. Richard Bach wrote: "Change our thought and the world around us changes." You can change the quality of your life by changing the context in which you view your circumstances. Two people can be faced with the same situation, such as being fired from a job; yet, one will view it as a blessing, and the other will view it as a curse. Changing the context of any situation depends on your ability to challenge the status quo, and think in broader terms.

Being single in a couples-crazed society means that you may be hassled by friends, acquaintances, co-workers, and relatives about your single status. They will pester you with questions about why you haven't married, and when you will eventually get married and have children. This happened to me when I worked for a large utility company for almost six years. People, who work for bureaucracies and follow the herd in everything they do in life, aren't

> *"Marriage is a bargain. And somebody has to get the worst of a bargain."*
>
> *- Helen Roland*

17

known for their ability to think in new ways. Because most people my age at the company were already married, I was often being asked to justify to them why I wasn't married. I am sure that if at that time I had been divorced twice - considered a two-time loser by some - I would have been considered more normal than someone who had never been married. In retrospect, there was nothing wrong with me. I never thought of it at the time, but I should have gone around asking all these married people to justify to me why they weren't single.

> *"I never cease being dumbfounded by the unbelievable things people believe."*
>
> *- Leo Rosten*

If anything, there is something wrong with married individuals who invariably follow the herd and can't accept anyone different. They must be somewhat insecure to believe that everyone should be like them. Perhaps, they are bored with their married lives, and are concerned that happy singles might be leading much more exciting and satisfying lives than married people.

A married person involved in family life isn't more successful than a single individual who doesn't have any children. Society's conviction to the superiority of marriage, along with parenthood, is just an addiction. The world will be a better place if all married and single individuals discard the belief that being married is good, and being unattached is bad.

Negative singles have accepted the erroneous belief that being married is better than being single. This belief is often hidden beneath several layers of habit and denial; a kind of conditioned blindness exists. Because they don't question society's beliefs, negative singles can become particular, rigid, and self-centered. These singles must rise above society's belief that something is wrong with them if they are single.

> *"Whatever deceives seems to produce a magical enchantment."*
>
> *- Plato*

It is easy to fall for false beliefs common in society. Here are two examples: Do you believe reading in the dark or poor light will hurt your eyes? Guess what? There is no evidence to support this. The American Academy of Ophthalmology states: "Reading in dim light can no more harm your eyes than taking a photograph in dim light can harm the camera."

Do you believe that it is dangerous to go swimming right after you eat a large meal? Here again, there is no evidence to support this. Although, the Red Cross published a brochure 50 years ago warning of the danger associated with eating before swimming, today's Red Cross brochure says it isn't dangerous to swim after eating.

Your Singles Advantage

- **You can sleep all night with the radio on**
- **The newspaper doesn't get all mixed up before you get to it**

Worse than having a false belief here and there is living a life based on what reality ought to be, instead of what it is. Writer Robert DeRopp stated that human beings inhabit a world of delusions, which obscures reality to such an extent that they are living in a world of waking dreams. The fear of the truth can be unshakable to certain individuals. People will go to great lengths to avoid the truth, and replace it with some wild fantasy that will make your brain spin.

Many unmotivated singles suffer from self-delusion about the existence of that Promised Land about halfway between Nirvana and Shangri-la; they believe that they can reach it without any effort. All it will take is one big deal in life in the form of a big lottery win, landing the ideal job, or finding the right marriage partner. The one-big-deal-in-life syndrome stems from false beliefs about the way the world ought to be, instead of the way it is. People suffering from the one-big-deal-in-life syndrome live a life based on part truth and part fiction. The fiction part entails what ought to be. Living a life based mainly on what the world ought to be, instead of the way it is, can be self-destructive; in fact, the consequences are usually quite severe.

Most of us have a tendency to structure our thinking patterns in ways which prevent us from seeing all the possibilities for finding solutions to life's problems. This tendency has a great impact on our creative abilities. Being a creative single means living with passion and spontaneity. Trusting your intuition is important; so is knowing when to suspend your preconceptions and inhibitions.

Flexible thinking will help you get through life with greater ease.

Don't get stuck in your beliefs. A belief, such as how much better life will be with marriage, is a disease. If you don't stop and question all your beliefs about life now and then, your structured thinking can be detrimental to your mental health. Structured thinking will limit your ability to see things in a different light. Remember, your mind is like a parachute - you are far better off when it is open.

I trust that you won't fall into the trap into which so many unmotivated people fall. Throughout their lives they suffer from the world-owes-me-a-living and windfall-from-nowhere syndromes. Assuming they don't have to take responsibility for their well-being, these people continually look for the easy way out. That's why so many North Americans are addicted to gambling, drugs, and alcohol. Most of us had the windfall-from-nowhere urge at one time or another. A long time ago, I used to imagine receiving windfalls from nowhere; now, this doesn't happen to me much, if at all. I realize that there is no such thing as a windfall from nowhere. Besides, I have found out that I don't need any windfall from nowhere to experience satisfaction and happiness in my life. I can accomplish this by using my creativity and following The Easy Rule Of Life.

So Who Are You?

Singles, who believe that being single is terrible, and having a marriage partner is wonderful, have a problem with their identities and self-esteem. Undoubtedly, as teenagers, we all at one time or another had self-esteem so low that we had to stand on our tip-toes, just so we could reach the bottom. Low self-esteem in teenagers is understandable. The problem is that many adult singles, with great natural ability, have been immobilized due to their inability to get their esteem out of the deep ditch where it rests; they have allowed the lack of a marriage partner to undermine their sense of self-worth.

People with low self-esteem tend to be extremely dependent upon others. They are unmotivated and have feelings of worthlessness. People with low self-esteem also may have the following symptoms or problems: anxiety, constant worry, guilt, fatigue, insomnia, unsubstantiated fears, poor health, feeling unattractive, inability to take criticism, and always wishing they could be happier.

"During sex I fantasize that I'm someone else."

- Richard Lewis

20

If you have even a hint of low self-esteem, it is imperative that you do what is necessary to get out of the rut, and raise your concept of yourself. With low self-esteem, you will continue to experience frustration and failure. Chronic low self-esteem can be a paralyzing disease which invariably produces emotional suffering and unhappiness.

Your Singles Advantage

- **No one has to find out you are a bad cook**
- **You always can listen to music you like**

Take a few moments in answering this simple question: Who are you? Being happy being single is knowing who you really are. Who you are should be your essence. Your essence is your character or your individuality. Your individuality makes you different from other people. If you have been in a lengthy relationship, you may take quite some time to find yourself. You have to stop defining yourself in terms of a relationship. Remember that even in relationships, everyone in reality is an individual or a "single" spending time with another individual or "single."

To find out who you are, look inside yourself for your own decisions, tastes, and interests. Don't let the concept of a partner or marriage become the only thing with meaning. Ensure that you develop hobbies and interests unrelated to marriage. Your self-image will then be something other than just a half of a couple. Listen to the intuitive voice within yourself, and not the conditioned voices of society. The best place to display your uniqueness is separate from a marriage partner. When you are asked who you are, most of your identity should be associated with your essence, which you display in pursuing your own personal interests.

The way to higher self-esteem is to change your attitude about the way things are, and the way you are. You shouldn't wait for your ship to come in; you should swim out to it. If you can start achieving something in your life, your

"Remember, no one can make you feel inferior without your consent."

- Eleanor Roosevelt

esteem is bound to go up. Achievements while you are single can be large or small; both will raise your esteem. With higher self-esteem, you will be more motivated to go out and get what you want in life. Because positive individuals are attracted to other positive people, you will attract more positive people in your life if you have a healthy attitude.

"Didn't you tell me that you were going to enroll in a course on self-esteem?"

"I didn't think that they would accept me."

Being single will be a blessing in disguise if you take the time to grow as a person, and if you don't tie your identity to being with another person. The day you wind up single through divorce or separation, is the day you get to test who you really are. Learning to enjoy being single involves the ability to experience everything through your own essence, instead of living vicariously through a spouse or partner.

If you have a poor self-image, no one but you can rescue you. Longing for someone special to come along and change how you feel about yourself isn't the answer. The answer is loving yourself first. If we don't love ourselves for who we are, it's hard to believe someone else will love us for who we are. You can best enjoy other people, and other people can enjoy you, when you enjoy and love yourself. Someone special is likely to enter your life only if you like yourself and think you deserve someone special.

Low self-esteem can be a major barrier to romance and a long-term relationship. If you feel you aren't in a relationship because you aren't intelligent, interesting, charismatic, or attractive enough to meet someone, you are undermining your chances for a relationship. Being happy single requires that you make peace with yourself. Self-esteem isn't dependent upon having amazing talents, great financial resources, or

"Nobody loves me like my mother, and she could be jivin', too."

- B. B. King

22

outstanding physical features. Having
self-esteem means feeling good about
yourself, having a positive attitude about what
you can attain in life, and how you are going to
get it.

> *"I was going to buy a copy of "The Power of Positive Thinking", and then I thought: "What the hell good would that do?"*
>
> *- Ronnie Shakes*

You can be confident and independent if
you overcome any feelings of inadequacy.
Give yourself recognition; pat yourself on the
back every so often. Mark Twain said: "If no
one gives you a compliment then give yourself one." Waiting for
others to give you recognition may make you feel very disappointed
when it doesn't come. Being self-confident and self-reliant allows
you to live happily as a single. Paradoxically, being self-confident
and self-reliant as a single increases the chances for your being in
an intimate relationship, if that is what you want. Self-confident
people, in tune with themselves and the world around them, tend to
attract other self-confident, in-tune individuals.

There is no easy or magical formula for making the best out of
being single. If you seek easy formulas to assist you, whether the
goal is losing weight, overcoming loneliness, making more money, or
having more leisure time, you are going to be extremely
disappointed. Giving up old habits is difficult; it takes effort and
energy. Nonetheless, spending all your time getting hung up on past
disappointments, present prejudices, and future worries won't
enhance your life. You must use your time in a creative and
productive manner to make single life work for you.

When you finally get over the need to be attached to someone
else, you will experience amazing contentment. You will wonder why
this feeling eluded you in the first place. You will be a winner when
you realize that being single is the true test of who you really are.
That is when you get to truly experience the joy of not being married.

Missing The Fantastic Relationship That Didn't Exist

If you have been in a long-term relationship, and are now
unattached, nostalgia for the relationship can overwhelm you at
times. One of the keys to being happy being single again is to
overcome whatever nostalgia you may experience for former

Your Singles Advantage

- **You can sleep diagonally on the king-size bed**
- **The TV remote control is all yours to command**

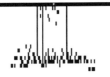

relationships. George W. Ball said: "Nostalgia is a seductive liar." When we think about something from the past, often we think about the good things, and forget the bad. We may remember that the relationship was fantastic, when, in fact, it was only good, or barely adequate. The worst case is people who reminisce about marvelous things that never happened. We tend to remember the good things about relationships, much more than the distasteful things that led to the break-up.

One way I have handled leaving any relationship is by thinking about the things I most disliked about the relationship, as well as other relationships in which I was involved. This quickly puts my being single in proper perspective. Whatever nostalgia I have for the relationship is quickly put to rest.

You can do the same when you miss your last relationship. Think about the negatives in the relationship. List the things you didn't like about it, including the daily boredom and the effort and energy required to keep it "working." Telling the truth about your last relationship may help you miss it less.

Divorced, separated, or never married - whatever your situation - you can be happy single. Being single doesn't mean being a loser. A single person doesn't have to spend the rest of life in discomfort and without purpose. Only ten percent of never-married individuals over the age of 40 will ever marry. Undoubtedly, the other 90 percent won't all live their lives in great discomfort or depression. In fact, many could marry, but choose not to for various personal reasons.

"Anyone who limits her vision to memories of yesterday is already dead."

- Lily Langtry

There are many disadvantages to being single. However, if one looks, one can find just as many disadvantages to being married. If you are recently separated, you must learn to let go of the past. Letting go means entering the unknown for self-discovery, and ultimately developing the confidence and security that you may have never had. The demands of single life dictate that you must rely on yourself to make your life work.

A new and exciting world exists out there for individuals without a partner. Being unattached allows you to enjoy life in a way not available to you when you are in a relationship. Not having to report to a spouse creates the ideal time to enjoy life like never before.

> *"Our disasters have been some of the best things that ever happened to us. And what we swore were blessings have been some of the worst."*
>
> *- From "One" By Richard Bach"*

"To Have A Friend, Be One"

A strong sense of community is essential to well-balanced, happy singles. There is a danger for singles to become socially isolated. To create a strong sense of community, it is important for singles to establish close and meaningful relationships with others. These relationships, although normally not as intimate as marital relationships, can provide the necessary ingredients for a sense of belonging and happiness. Family and friends can be a source of this social network necessary for support and companionship.

Freud said love and work make people happy. Love has many dimensions. It is assumed that intimate relationships are the only source of love and happiness. Love in an intimate relationship certainly contributes to happiness and makes life worthwhile. However, intimate relationships aren't the only source of happiness. Many of the world's highly creative people who don't have intimate interpersonal relationships lead extremely happy lives. These people aren't loners or antisocial. They are social people who have satisfying close relationships, but less intimate ones, with others. They also have a passion for their work, or an important purpose in life. These creative single people attain happiness and lead worthwhile lives based on a mixture of close relationships and satisfying vocations.

Singles shouldn't just focus on friends with the same philosophy and lifestyle. As a single person, you may be able to develop a wider

> *"Men and women who have affection for one another should live close to each other, and visit occasionally."*
>
> *- Katherine Hepburn*

Your Singles Advantage

- **You always have the final say on the temperature setting in your home**
- **It is easier to have many friends**

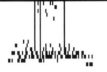

variety of friends than married people. You have an opportunity to meet a diverse range of personalities with an interesting assortment of interests and tastes.

There is a big difference between friends and acquaintances. In his book *"Illusions,"* Richard Bach wrote: "Your friends will know you better in the first minute you meet than your acquaintances will know you in a thousand years." Close relationships are based on self-disclosure, affection, and trust. Business associates or golfing buddies are not necessarily close friends. These relationships are normally based on goal orientation and competitiveness which don't lead to true friendship. A close friend is someone who will provide emotional support when needed. He or she is someone you can talk to about personal matters, and whose opinion you will solicit and consider when making an important decision.

Close relationships with friends and relatives are also essential for easing some of the less serious problems in life. Close relationships will do you a world of good. Friends will cost you virtually nothing in financial terms. There will be a cost - your time along with your own willingness to share yourself and offer assistance from time to time.

"True happiness ... arises, in the first place from the enjoyment of one's self, and in the next, from the friendship and conversation of a few select companions."

- Joseph Addison

When with friends, avoid the excessive need to persuade them of your own beliefs or strong points of view. You will notice that participating in the game of who is right and who is wrong is normally a waste of time and energy. Winning an argument often doesn't convince the other person that your point of view is right, no matter how logical your argument is. If you want to convince people that your philosophy and points of view are "right," then convince them by action. Do you want

26

to change the world for the better in some way based on your strong convictions? If the answer is yes, then make this your purpose in life. Then embrace your purpose and "run with it." When you accomplish incredible feats by following your convictions, others will take note. Well-balanced people will be convinced of your stand, and even a few skeptical people will come around to your point of view.

> *"Tell me thy company, and I'll tell thee what thou art."*
>
> *- Miguel de Cervantes*

Announcing all your problems to everyone you encounter in the course of a day will destroy your chances of attracting positive people. Paradoxically, these are the people who can best help you, and give you optimistic support and advice on how to solve your problems. Positive people, with their healthy attitudes and personal accomplishments, exude the encouragement that you need to solve important problems.

Of course, it is much easier to attract enthusiastic people when you yourself are enthusiastic. Being distrustful of everyone, and pessimistic about the world, won't help you attract quality people. You will have to show respect, affection, and good humor in your dealings with others if you expect the same in return.

Invest energy in your friendships and the rewards will be amazingly satisfying. Good friends will be there when you need them for support and entertainment, if you are there for them when they need you. As Longfellow said: "To have a friend, be one."

The Company You Keep Reflects Your Character

You have heard this before: keep things simple; sticking to the basics makes life a lot easier and more satisfying. Nonetheless, for some mysterious reason, most people go to great lengths to complicate their lives. One area is in the company they keep.

Life is much easier if you don't carry excess baggage. Negative people are excess baggage you can't afford to carry. On an airline, excess baggage will cost you money. Negative people will cost you much more than money. The price will be your time, energy,

> *"Associate yourself with men of good quality if you esteem your own reputation, for tis better to be alone than in bad company."*
>
> *- George Washington*

27

and happiness. Negative people can even cost you your sanity in the end. A total crash of your mental stability can happen if you surround yourself with too many negative people. At best, you won't succeed in your goals and projects which are important to your happiness and satisfaction.

> *"One was never married and that's his hell; another is, and that's his plague."*
>
> *- Robert Barton*

Negative people will seek your support for their notion that the world is a lousy place. Nothing irks negative and unmotivated people more than individuals who are positive and successful. It is important that you spot and avoid people who are likely to drain your energy. If you have friends or acquaintances who are constantly depressed and complaining about life, their negative energy will sap your positive energy. Don't spend a great deal of time with people who have a negative attitude, unless their state of mind is temporary due to some serious problem. It is in your best interests to avoid negative people as much as possible.

No doubt you have heard the joke about the drunk who was lying in the gutter where a pig had also stopped to rest. A woman happened to walk by and said aloud: "You can judge one's character by the company one keeps." The pig promptly got up and walked away. Another mistake some individuals make is to hang around with lazy and negative people because they get to look like geniuses in the eyes of this company. The problem is the rest of the world, like the lady in the joke, judges you by the company you keep.

Don't make the mistake of trying to change negative people, expecting their imminent transformation into more positive individuals. In his book *"One,"* Richard Bach wrote: "No one can solve problems for someone whose problem is that they don't want problems solved." In case you haven't learned, negative people don't change. If they do, it is only after a lengthy period, time which you can't afford. Instead of expending your energy trying to change someone, utilize that energy in changing yourself for the better.

> *"The best time to make friends is before you need them."*
>
> *- Ethel Barrymore*

Surround yourself with enthusiastic people who have positive things to say about life. Enthusiastic people have an inner fire and an incredible zest for living that are irresistible. Their radiance and zest for living create an energy field which anyone in the vicinity is sure to feel. You can learn a lot from positive people. They have acquired a great deal of wisdom and knowledge about life. If nothing else, common sense tells us to surround ourselves with highly motivated individuals, instead of people who rob us of our energy.

Being Too Nice Can Be A Sign Of A Boring Person

A woman recently wrote a letter to Ann Landers asking for advice on how to respond to the antics of her mother-in-law. The mother-in-law drove her crazy because she continually borrowed things which she didn't return. Three years after a crockpot was lent, it still hadn't been returned. A typewriter was returned briefly upon request, and then taken again and never returned. The concerned woman was afraid to say anything because she wanted to stay on good terms with her mother-in-law, who was otherwise in her words "a wonderful person." The problem with this concerned woman is that she is so obsessed with being liked that she puts herself through emotional turmoil. Ann Landers appropriately gave this advice to the woman: "This is going to be a lifelong problem unless you replace the spaghetti in your spine with a backbone."

"Do you think that I am boring?"

"I know that we have met, but who the heck are you?"

Don't let the urge to be nice to everyone interfere with your willingness to take risks and enjoy life. Having the urge to be nice to everyone translates into wanting to be liked by everyone. Robin Chandler, a British actor, states: "The disease of niceness cripples more lives than alcoholism. Nice people are simply afraid to say no, are constantly worrying about what others think of them, constantly adapting their behavior to please - never getting to do what they want to do."

Being too nice can hurt your career. A common problem with male and female managers at all corporate levels who are failing in their jobs is that they are too nice. "I'm one of those people who lives to be loved. My inability to deal with conflict was ripping my group apart" were the words of an executive cited by *Fortune* magazine. He was on the verge of being fired because he was Mr. Nice Guy. The morale in his department was extremely low due to his inability to make tough decisions. It took a year of outside counseling for him to come to the conclusion: "You hurt people more if you can't give them constructive feedback." After this executive toughened his manner, and developed the courage to fire people, the morale of his group rose.

> "If you have no enemies, you are apt to be in the same predicament in regard to friends."
>
> - Elbert Hubbard

A good target group on which to practice not being nice is home telephone solicitors. Don't feel guilty if you cause a few telephone solicitors to quit their jobs. (We can use a lot fewer home telephone solicitors - the optimum number we should strive for is zero.) As Ann Landers recently wrote in response to a telephone solicitor who complained about people who were rude to him: "If you're looking for sympathy, you dialed the wrong number ...... the telephone is a convenience for which customers pay. No one should disturb their eating, sleeping, bathing, love making, or whatever with a sales pitch."

Your Singles Advantage

- **You can squeeze the toothpaste in the middle and leave the cap off without anyone getting mad**

Being too nice can also undermine your chances for a meaningful relationship. If you are afraid to object to being treated badly or unfairly because you are afraid of losing your girlfriend or boyfriend, you will end up resenting her or him. This situation may eventually have greater consequences than if you confront your partner with your objections and expectations. Sociologist Diane Felmlee surveyed 300 people and found that 29 percent reported that in past relationships what they had first considered a virtue in their partner eventually became a flaw. One important virtue that became a liability was the trait of being nice. It appears that "nice"

marriage partners became very boring. This is probably because nice people have at least some of the typical traits of boring people.

Being Bored Is An Insult To Oneself

Many singles profess that handling boredom is their greatest source of anxiety. If they are not married, engaged, or otherwise coupled, they feel that they are wasting their lives. Free time is something they fear because they feel an intimate relationship is needed to overcome boredom. They don't use their time effectively, and happiness escapes them. Instead of being participants in life, they specialize in being spectators and critics of other people's activities. Singlehood becomes one continuous period of boredom and dejection. Boredom deprives people of the meaning of life and undermines their zest for living. Although it would seem to specifically affect those who are single or jobless, working and married people can be just as susceptible.

Being a spectator isn't the way to get the most out of being single. You can't sit around and expect exciting things to happen to you. Only you can take responsibility for situating yourself in places where something is likely to happen. By planning and using your time wisely, you will be able to experience old and new activities which enhance the quality of your life.

> *"I am never bored anywhere: being bored is an insult to oneself."*
>
> *- Jules Renard*

Keeping busy doing the things you love will help you handle boredom. Taking on new and difficult tasks helps conquer boredom. You must be accountable for your boredom. Following is the complete content from a letter that I received from a professor in the Faculty of Education at a university in Western Canada:

Dear Mr. Zelinski

I very much enjoyed your book, "The Joy Of Not Working". I decided that I am boring myself; I plan to do something about it."

Thank you

John

> *"A gossip is one who talks to you about others, a bore is one who talks to you about himself; and a brilliant conversationalist is one who talks to you about yourself."*
>
> *- Lisa Kirk*

From several hundred letters that I received about *"The Joy Of Not Working,"* this letter is one of the most powerful, despite being the shortest. The chapter on boredom titled *Somebody Is Boring Me, I Think It Is Me* must have made an impact on John. He realized that there is only one person in his life who can do something about his boredom - John!

Psychologists have determined that people who are chronically bored are conformists, worriers, lacking self-confidence, uncreative, highly sensitive to criticism, and anxious for security and material things. Boredom is most likely to hit people who choose the safer, no-risk path in life. Because they take no risks, they seldom reap the payoffs of accomplishment, contentment, and satisfaction. People who choose the path of variety and stimulation are rarely stricken with the ailment of boredom. Creative individuals, who look for many things to do, and many ways of doing them, find that life is tremendously exciting and worthwhile.

In modern times, boredom is thought to be externally imposed. However, the failure of our imaginations leads us into boredom. Things become boring because we expect them to be stimulating. People who require novelty in all their external activities are undoubtedly addicted to novelty. Due to their lack of imaginative thinking, many of these people try to evade the dullness of their daily lives by gambling, drinking, and taking drugs. People addicted to novelty are known to change jobs, marriage partners, and surroundings with reckless abandon. Because they don't use their imaginations, they continually wind up bored and dissatisfied.

> *"When you're bored with yourself, marry and be bored with someone else."*
>
> *- David Pryce-Jones*

Perfectionists, who set unrealistically high standards for life, are prime candidates for boredom, and even depression. They set these extremely high standards for their friends and themselves. Everything in life is supposed to be exciting and interesting. Perfectionists tend to set these standards for prospective marriage partners. If these prospective partners don't turn out to be charming, exceptionally attractive, and interesting, perfectionists get bored with these men or women; they eventually reject them because they are too boring, failing to recognize that the fault is with themselves.

> *"Friendship with oneself is all important because without it one cannot be friends with anyone else."*
>
> *- Eleanor Roosevelt*

We must confront our boredom whenever it strikes. Only by using our imaginations can we overcome boredom. Your willingness to take responsibility for your boredom is the creative force which will determine whether you enjoy being single. Once you have accepted that your attitude determines the quality of your life, you are well on your way to eliminating boredom and dejection.

Developing A Relationship With The Most Important Person In Your Life

Never challenging the way we think about marriage and being single has the inherent danger of getting ourselves plugged into one way of thinking, without seeing other alternatives which may be more appropriate. If you presently have no partner with whom to share your life, there are a number of alternatives. It is up to you to create and enjoy those alternatives. The notion that anyone needs a partner to survive and enjoy life is false. Making the most out of being single requires that you develop a positive relationship with the most important person in your life - you!

Effective transition to single life will require that you transform your identity, maintain high self-esteem, acquire new friends, and develop fresh interests. If you haven't exercised for years, start now. Your health will be enhanced both mentally and physically. Writing and other inner creative pursuits can be effective ways to develop your individuality. Pursue interests and activities which you have always wanted to pursue, but may not have had the opportunity to pursue in the past.

> *"It is not easy to find happiness in ourselves, and it is not possible to find it elsewhere."*
>
> *- Agnes Repplier*

Unlike just a decade or two ago, being single today doesn't mean being a social misfit. Millions of people who comprise the singles community have similar experiences.

Your Singles Advantage

- **You can put ketchup on your popcorn without a spouse nagging you**
- **You don't have to listen to a marriage partner's bad jokes**

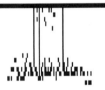

These singles have many expectations and aspirations in common. The singles lifestyle offers a great deal of opportunity for individuals who want to explore and make the best of this lifestyle. The number of options for self-discovery available to the single person is unlimited.

Single individuals can experience the world in ways unavailable to married people. Many singles find being unattached most desirable because they can live life to its full potential from an individual point of view. Ironically, they are enhancing their chances for a meaningful relationship because they are relaxed and in-tune with themselves.

Mark Twain said: "The worst loneliness is not to be comfortable with yourself." High-flying singles are comfortable with themselves. Unlike many singles who wouldn't be caught dead in a restaurant or coffee bar by themselves, positive singles have no hang-ups about attending functions alone. People who are happy being single have developed a certain attitude and self-sufficiency about life and its opportunities for the single person.

The singles experience offers a big challenge for the motivated who like variety and freedom in their lives, and don't believe they have to follow the herd at every turn. Creatively alive singles look at being single as a privilege or luxury; they have created a singles paradise. Well-balanced singles are married to their independence. They feel good about themselves and aren't paralyzed because they have no marriage partner. These positive people know that their source of happiness lies within themselves. Being single is an opportunity for personal growth and a time for adventure.

"To love oneself is the beginning of a lifelong romance."

- Oscar Wilde

34

3. Marriage: All The Ingredients Of A Greek Tragedy?

Thinking About Marriage

In a letter quoted in an officially approved biography, Prince Charles is reported to have written: "It has all the ingredients of a Greek tragedy. I never thought it would end up like this .... how could I have got it all so wrong?" Prince Charles' reflection on his failed marriage to Princess Diana provides some food for thought. Do people get married for the wrong reasons? Many, like Charles and Diana, apparently do.

The majority of the British, Canadian, and American public were surprised to learn that the Royal Family's marriages are just as rocky as those of the general population. Tantamount to believing in the infallibility of the Royal Family is believing in Santa Claus and other fairy tales. Also associated with believing in Santa Claus and other fairy tales is thinking about how great

> "By all means marry; if you get a good wife, you'll be happy. If you get a bad one, you'll become a philosopher."
>
> - Socrates

it will be when we get married. Many of us dream about how much better things will be when we can finally share our lives with someone. A couples-crazed society influences us to believe that marriage and ultimate happiness are one and the same. Through movies, magazines, and novels, we have been programmed to believe in Prince Charming meeting Cinderella and, of course, living happily ever after.

Fantasy and reality give somewhat contradictory messages about marriage. Lifelong marriage is supposed to mean a life with fulfillment through enjoyable and rewarding activities. It is supposed to be the great escape from the stresses inherent in single life. As in the case of Prince Charles, marriage doesn't always live up to people's expectations.

> *"The trouble with some women is that they get excited about nothing - and then marry him."*
>
> *- Cher*

If you want to enhance the quality of your single life, challenging your thoughts about marriage, and what constitutes happiness in life, is a good place to start. To challenge your own values and attitudes about marriage and single life, answer the questions in the following exercise. Try to focus your thinking in other directions than you might normally take.

Exercise: - Something To Think About

Do you think that research studies conclude that single people aren't as happy as married people?

Does divorce mean failure?

Should society encourage people to get married?

Should people marry someone they don't love for the purpose of having children or acquiring a means for economic survival?

Should people settle for less than they expect in a marriage?

There are no right answers to the above questions. This exercise is meant only to challenge your values and attitudes about marriage. Your ability to enjoy single life to the fullest will depend on how flexible you are in your views. If you are able to question all your conservative and traditional values, and put the outdated ones to sleep, you will come into your own as a person. Regardless of your situation in life, you will find more enjoyment just from being able to have a more positive perspective about singlehood, and the quality of life that is possible while being unattached.

> *"All marriages are happy. It's the living together afterward that causes all the trouble."*
>
> *- Raymond Hull*

Note that even happily married people miss single life to some degree. Typically, the reply from a married individual yearning for single life will be something like this: "I used to be well read and in great physical shape before marriage. Now I am coping with a wife who says I don't spend enough time with her, three kids, working sixty hours a week, visiting friends, relatives and in-laws, and running errands all weekend. I don't have even a minute for myself for the things I really love to do."

In response to a survey by *Men's Health* magazine about what its readers want in life, one man wrote: "I'd like a clause in my marriage vows that allows me to be single one week a year." Many married individuals, even happily married ones, miss some aspects of single life. While talking to happily married people, I discovered they miss the following things:

Your Singles Advantage

- **No obnoxious in-laws to cope with**
- **You aren't answerable to anyone**

What Married People Miss About Being Single

* Time to read
* Time to participate in activities such as bicycling and tennis
* Single friends who they have stopped seeing
* Time for solitude
* More room to create personal space
* Being able to write, nap, meditate .... etc. without being disturbed

For truly happily married individuals, marriage is a blessing. The key ingredients are sharing, intimacy, support, communication, accommodation, and companionship. Pleasant experiences include initial sensations of mutual attraction, playing and laughing together, wild times in bed, get-togethers with friends and

"When a man opens a car door for his wife, it's either a new car or a new wife."

- Prince Philip

> *"Marriage is the only evil that men pray for."*
>
> *- Greek Proverb*

relatives, accumulation of mutual property, and the satisfaction of raising children. A happy and successful long-term marriage is a way to discover life's secrets with someone special. Some marriages like those below have lasted longer than most.

Long Hollywood Marriages

♥ Bob Hope and Dolores Reade have been married for over 60 years.

♥ Jane Wyatt and Edgar Bethune Ward have been married for 59 years.

♥ Charlton Heston and Lydia Clarke have been married for 51 years.

Although the government hasn't outlawed long-lasting marriages such as those above, they are increasingly rare. The divorce rate indicates how dangerous it is to look to marriage as a guaranteed road to happiness and fulfillment. In 1993, the U.S. Census Bureau forecast that four out of ten first marriages will end up on the rocks.

Besides the freedom to come and go, there are many things that singles have to give up when they get married. The sacrifices needed for marriage would be worth it if marriage was guaranteed to provide long-term fulfillment. Alas, after all the sacrifices, many marriages still fall apart. In the U.S., during the last decade and a half, for every two couples who have married one couple has divorced. No wonder more people than ever aren't bothering to ever get married.

> *"To reduce stress, avoid excitement. Spend more time with your spouse."*
>
> *- Robert Orben*

Being unattached can be a tragedy; so can being attached. Marriage is supposed to be a cure-all event which enhances our lives dramatically. Getting married should give us the life that we have always contemplated in our dreams. Not all evidence supports the notion that marriage leads to Nirvana. Certainly, one would have to be totally oblivious not to realize that marriage isn't a panacea for loneliness and dejection.

Economic And Other Questionable Reasons For Marriage

Some sociologists believe that North Americans marry strictly for economic, political, and social reasons. Anthropologist Helen Fisher disputes this, and suggests that many North Americans may marry to enhance their inner selves. In her book *"Anatomy Of Love,"* she states: "We marry for love and to accentuate, balance out, or mask parts of our private lives." Fisher may be right about some North Americans, but not all. People are different; they marry for a variety of reasons. Here are some of them:

Reasons Why People Marry

* To have children
* To establish financial security
* To satisfy parents or friends
* Expectations of great intimacy
* To overcome boredom
* For the ceremony
* To overcome loneliness
* To have plentiful sex
* To experience success vicariously through one's mate
* To get over a previous marriage or relationship
* To share one's life with another person
* To have someone else solve one's problems
* To experience the well-being of living with another person
* To have an attractive partner
* Guaranteed fidelity - to have a faithful partner
* Society's norms - belief that couples are more valued than singles

> "It was so cold I almost got married."
>
> - Shelly Winters

Some of the above reasons are positive; others are negative, or questionable. Psychologist Michael Broder in his book *"The Art Of Living Single"* lists positive and negative reasons for wanting an intimate relationship with someone. A marriage based on positive reasons is characterized by desire, and not on fear or need. His positive reasons for getting into relationships include the desire for sexual enjoyment, the well-being that comes from enjoyment of a partner's company, and the satisfaction that comes from sharing one's life with someone.

A negative reason for marrying is one based on fear or need. People, who marry due to fear or need, will fulfill only some of their unsatisfied desires. Broder identifies six negative reasons for marrying. Five of the negative reasons are to overcome loneliness, to increase self-esteem, to satisfy the belief that couples are more valued than singles, to make a former marriage partner jealous, and to help get over the last relationship.

> *"Don't marry a man to reform him - that's what reform schools are for."*
>
> *- Mae West*

Money invariably seems to come into the picture whenever marriage is involved. This may surprise many people, but the sixth negative reason Broder identifies for being in a relationship is "the need to establish financial security." Going through with a marriage with a person one doesn't love, just to acquire financial security, isn't a productive thing to do in the long run. Marrying for the sole purpose of establishing financial security will only mask one's pain temporarily. It certainly won't contribute to a happy and solid long-term relationship.

> *"Women deceived by men, want to marry them; it is a kind of revenge as good as any other."*
>
> *- Phillippe De Remi Beaunonoir*

The reality is some people marry strictly for money. A recent survey showed that nine percent of women in the United States are willing to marry a wealthy man they don't love. Anyone about to marry someone well-off to acquire financial security should give the issue of money and marriage more thought. The same applies to someone well-off who is offering someone financial security by marrying him or her. More discussion about money and relationships is presented in Chapter 9.

Too Much Intimacy Can Be Harmful To A Marriage

The search for intimacy is one of the main reasons people marry. Ironically, the search for intimacy may be why many marriages fail. The preoccupation with intimacy as the source of true happiness is a fairly recent phenomenon for human beings. Generations before us were too busy earning a living and pursuing other interests, instead of striving for a great deal of intimacy, let alone perfect intimacy.

The stability in marriages has been undermined due to the exaggerated expectations people have for them. In his book, *"Solitude,"* Anthony Storr makes the statement: "If we did not look to marriage as the principal source of happiness, fewer marriages would end in tears." Storr, a British psychiatrist, believes that interests, beyond relationships, help define healthy identities and give meaning to lives. People need sources of fulfillment beyond their intimate relationships. According to Storr, what goes on in people's minds when they are alone is central to achieving fulfillment. The capacity to be alone reflects a basic security, which becomes increasingly important with the aging process.

Psychologist Geraldine K. Piorkowski, writing in the January/ February, 1995 issue of *Psychology Today* magazine, warns about people's expectations of intimacy in marriage. She states that people's preoccupation with relationships leads them to demand too much intimacy. This has a negative impact. People looking for a moderate amount of intimacy will be much happier than people looking for a great deal of intimacy, or perfect intimacy. She states that our preoccupation with intimacy is unnatural.

Piorkowski further states that unmitigated intimacy isn't only difficult to achieve, but it can be harmful as well. The problem is that many people place too many emotional demands on intimate relationships. They expect their marriage partner to be not only a lover, but a friend, companion, playmate, and parent. These expectations, rooted in our culture, have people looking to their marriage partners as solutions for all their problems.

These unrealistic expectations of marriage partners contribute to the high divorce rate. Many people end up thinking their partners are inadequate when they don't live up to their expectations. Piorkowski cites evidence

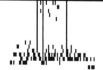

Your Singles Advantage

- **You can jog in your living room**
- **You can eat pizza every day for a whole month**
- **There are no messy problems of family life**

"Are you married?"　　　*"Occasionally!"*

indicating a limit to the amount of intimacy well-balanced partners can tolerate. Healthy individuals need solitude for creativity and productivity.

Much of what Piorkowski says supports Antony Storr's claims. People have to allow more time to recharge themselves. They should get involved in more close, but nonromantic relationships, as well as other activities such as learning new things, spiritual development, and solving the world's social ills. Looking to marriage as a source of all satisfaction and happiness can be detrimental to the marriage.

The Queen-For-A-Day Trap

For the longest time I couldn't figure out why several of my former girlfriends, who hadn't talked to me for over a year or two, telephoned to let me know that they were getting married. In most cases, they didn't even invite me to the wedding. They all did say that they wanted to see me after the wedding to have coffee or play tennis. In virtually all of the cases, I didn't hear from them again. Somewhere along the way, I became perplexed by this rather odd behavior. I was puzzled by why these women called to let me know that they were getting married, considering that I hadn't heard from any of them for over a year or two.

This was before I read about the queen-for-a-day theory. This theory is as good an explanation as any other I could create by myself. To many women, much more than men, the wedding in itself is just as important as the chance to experience married life. This is especially true for young, single women who constantly dream about marriage and the wedding itself, because they are conditioned to want it. Men, on the other hand, don't grow up thinking or dreaming about the wedding and being a groom. The young bride is the center of attention for three or four weeks preceding the ceremony. She ends up being the envy of many female acquaintances up until, and including, the ceremony. In contrast, the groom gets little extra attention in the few weeks preceding his wedding.

Because of the attention, some women want the wedding as much, if not more, than married life. The wedding shows the world that they have been successful in achieving their marriage goals. That is why my former girlfriends, whom I haven't seen for a while, keep telephoning me just before they get married - to let me know that they have been successful in their marriage goals. To many women, the trip to the altar means that they get to be queen-for-a-day. Take, for example, Celine Dion, who in 1994 at the age of 26 married her longtime manager, Rene Angelil, 51 at the time. The media reported that the wedding reception cost $500,000, and was the Quebec show-business equivalent to a royal wedding. I doubt very much that Angelil wanted a $500,000 wedding, considering that this was his third marriage. Of the glitzy ceremony, Celine Dion stated: "It's the show of my life." Another example is the Wayne Gretzky and Janet Jones wedding which also cost a king's ransom. I almost would be willing to bet a king's ransom that Janet Jones wanted the expensive wedding more than Wayne Gretzky.

> *"Marrying a man is like buying something you've been admiring for a long time in a shop window. You may love it when you get it home, but it doesn't always go with everything else in the house."*
>
> *- Jean Kerr*

The point is getting married just for the chance to get to be queen-for-a-day (or to be king-for-a-day if any man desires this) is a poor reason by itself for getting married. Getting married because parents and society expect it is also a silly reason. If people are truly in love, and want to get married, then they should. A ceremony, especially a glitzy, expensive ceremony, shouldn't be necessary. Glitzy and expensive ceremonies indicate how much importance people place on satisfying and impressing others that they have been successful at the game of marriage.

> *"Any intelligent woman who reads the marriage contract, and then goes into it, deserves all the consequences."*
>
> *- Isadora Duncan*

Some time ago, Helen Lawrenson wrote in *Esquire* magazine: "Very few modern women either like or desire marriage, especially after the ceremony has been performed. Primarily women wish attention and affection.

Your Singles Advantage

- **You don't have to pretend to be cheerful when you aren't**
- **You don't have to wait for the washroom**

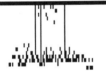

Matrimony is something they accept when there is no alternative." The problem is if a woman marries for the ceremony and to be a queen-for-a-day, she may not be considering all the other essential elements which make for a successful marriage. After the ceremony, the marriage may rapidly go downhill.

Marrying For Children - A Questionable Ancient Ritual

The opportunity to have and raise children is one of the main reasons why people get married. Marrying young to have children is a ritual which has been around for thousands of years. A century or so ago, it was necessary for poor, farming couples to marry early, and have many children so that there would be more workers in the fields. Coupling early and having several children is an ancient tribal value that made sense at one time. Today, it makes little sense, but is still followed by many people in Western cultures.

We are destroying our environment through economic and population growth. In February of 1994, a study presented by ecologists to the American Advancement of Science's conference in San Francisco concluded that the present population of six billion has to fall by 67 percent to around two billion in order that people can be sustained in relative comfort. If current growth rates are maintained, the earth's population will reach between twelve billion and fifteen billion by the year 2100. The idea that the greatest purpose we can have in life is to get married so we can raise children undoubtedly will have to be questioned more and more in the future.

"People who say they sleep like a baby usually don't have one."

- Leo J. Burke

I don't know the perfect way to control population. There are certainly many possibilities if we are serious about solving the problem. It certainly isn't by encouraging people to get married for the primary purpose of having more children. It is apparent that individuals who don't have children are making an important contribution to a greener world. Married or single people who don't have children are doing this world a great favor. If the world continues to deteriorate at the present pace due to overpopulation, society may have to pay a bonus to people who don't have children. In light of the population problem, singles and married people not having children may be considered to make a greater contribution to society than couples who have children. For the world to survive, the childless couple may have to be the rule rather than the exception.

> *"The couple is the most selfish entity in the world."*
>
> *- Unknown Wise Person (quoted in Washington Post Magazine)*

Blaming the overpopulation problem on Third World countries as some North Americans do is shunning responsibility. A child born in North America will consume 23 times as much in natural resources as a child in the Third World. A couple having three children in North America has the same effect on the depletion of the natural resources as ten couples having a total of 69 children in the Third World. Scientists say that if everyone in the world tried to live at the same level as people in North America, half of the world would starve to death.

Do childless married people have to be less happy than married people with children? It is a fallacy that older people who have never had children are lonelier, or less happy, than people with children. Carin Smith, editor of the quarterly newsletter *Childless By Choice*, was quoted in the October, 1994 edition of *New Choices* magazine as saying: "The vast majority of older people without kids do not feel alone or have regrets. In fact, more than ten percent of all women over sixty have never had children and many couldn't be happier."

> *When asked why he did not become a father, Thales answered "Because I am fond of children."*
>
> *- Diogenes Laertius*

Till Infidelity And Boredom Us Do Part

Two more reasons why people marry are to have plentiful sex and to have a faithful partner. In theory, both of these reasons are great; in practice, both are questionable. Conventional wisdom dictates sex is so plentiful and great in most marriages that only singles with no access to sex - or people in lousy marriages - practice masturbation. *Sex in America*, an extensive study on sexual practices and attitudes, conducted by three U.S. university sociologists and a *New York Times* writer, contradicts conventional wisdom. The report, published in the fall of 1994, stated: "Nearly 85 percent of men and 45 percent of women who were living with a sexual partner said they had masturbated in the past year." The survey found that married people were significantly more likely to masturbate than people who were living alone.

"Marriage is not a word but a sentence."

- Unknown Wise Person

You may be surprised that married people masturbate more than single people. What is the reason for this? Optimistically, it could mean that sexually active people like doing a variety of things, instead of just one, and that masturbation just compliments and enhances sex. Realistically, it may be that familiar and regular sex in marriage is so lousy that even masturbation is better. It could also mean that sex isn't so plentiful, and masturbation is a good substitute.

Sex in many marriages hasn't been plentiful and great for some time. In the sixties, a group of individuals formed the Sex Information and Education Council of the United States (SIECUS), because one in two marriages was warped by sexual problems. According to a 1979 SIECUS fund raising letter, sex in marriages was shrouded by fear, guilt, and bigotry along with many misconceptions, and had to be brought out into the limelight if the U.S. was to overcome its sex problems.

The sex problems in intimate relationships still persist. In a survey conducted by the Roper Organization, only 50 percent of men said they were very satisfied with their sex lives, and 44 percent thought their partners were satisfied. Only 56 percent of women said they were very satisfied, and 60 percent of women thought their partners were. This means that 50 percent of men and 44 percent of women aren't very satisfied with their sex lives.

A story, which I heard on CBC radio's Basic Black, about Mrs. Coolidge's sex problems with her husband, the thirtieth president of the U.S., leads us into infidelity. Calvin Coolidge wasn't considered by his wife to be very sexually active. One day, his wife was on a visit to a farm with the President's personal assistant. She noticed a rooster which seemed unusually sexually active. She learned that the rooster performed several times a day. Mrs. Coolidge instructed the assistant to: "Go tell this to Mr. Coolidge."

The assistant relayed this important information to the President and told him that Mrs. Coolidge had asked him to do so. Amazed by the rooster's ability to perform several times a day, Mr. Coolidge asked the assistant: "Does the rooster do this with the same hen?" The assistant replied: "Of course not - it's with a different hen every time." Mr. Coolidge responded with: "Go tell that to Mrs. Coolidge."

"I just learned that our new neighbor Mr. Klipson makes love to his wife twice a day. Why don't you do that?"

"Give me a little time. I haven't even met her yet!"

Like the rooster, some people find sex more exciting and plentiful if there are more partners involved. People choose monogamous relationships expecting their partner to be sexually faithful. The reality is that infidelity is quite common in monogamous relationships; a fair number of married North Americans share their sexual energy with more than one person.

Monogamy is normal, but so is infidelity. This appears to be a contradiction, but the definition of monogamy by itself doesn't imply a state of total fidelity. The dictionary definition of monogamy is typically: "the condition or custom of being married to one person at a time." Monogamy doesn't indicate that a marriage partner is always faithful.

"Your wife has been cheating on us."

- Words in a country song

A recent *Flair* magazine survey indicated that 29 percent of its readers cheated on their spouses. Other surveys indicate different numbers for the cheaters. One thing is certain: North American men and women philander. What is uncertain is the number; the results of surveys vary so widely that it is hard to settle on accurate numbers.

People have affairs for other reasons than sex. The *Flair* magazine survey cited above indicated that 41 percent of those who cheat on their spouses cite physical attraction as the reason. Another 20 percent said that they cheat due to the influence of drugs and alcohol, and 16 percent cheat for revenge. Here are some of the many reasons that men and women give for having affairs:

> *"I think a man can have two, maybe three affairs while he is married. But three is the absolute maximum. After that, you are cheating."*
>
> *- Yves Montand*

Why People Have Affairs

* Overpowering experience of lust
* Searching for more intimacy
* To feel special
* Add excitement to life
* Want sexual variety
* Establish more independence
* Prove that they are wanted by someone else
* Revenge for something that spouse has done
* Marriage partner is not interested in sex
* To overcome dullness in a mediocre marriage

Nothing will be more effective than an affair by a partner in quashing the experience of love, including a lack of sexual interest by one's partner, lying by the partner, or the partner not paying enough attention. Infidelity causes serious problems in a relationship; often the result is divorce once the innocent partner finds out. For men, infidelity leads to another danger: *Longevity Magazine* (January 1995) reported that studies indicate as many as 13 percent of all children may not be fathered by the men who think that they are the real fathers.

> *"Mothers are fonder than fathers of their children because they are more certain they are their own."*
>
> *- Aristotle*

How much is fidelity worth to a marriage when money is available for the taking? After the release of the Demi Moore-Robert Redford movie *Indecent Proposal*, the Roper Organization surveyed 504 people to find out how much being faithful was worth. Of the 504 people, 7.5 percent said that they would sleep, or let their partner sleep, with another person for $1,000,000. Another 13 percent of respondents said that they didn't know, or refused to answer. This could mean that 15 to 20 percent of married people are prepared to have a third party engage in sexual activities with them or their spouses for $1,000,000.

Your Singles Advantage

- **No conflict if you meet someone new and fall in love tomorrow**
- **No need to have a joint bank account with anyone**

Note that not all people who seek out affairs are necessarily in dull relationships. Individuals who claim to be in a happy relationship are known to have affairs, even though they are risking their relationship, emotional stability, and careers. Although infidelity causes pain and guilt for the parties involved, affairs are common. It appears that something goes wrong with most relationships at one time or another, if the results of a survey, published in the June 1, 1987 issue of *Marriage and Divorce Today*, are even close to being accurate. The results indicate that 70 percent of all married Americans have taken part in an affair during their marital life.

The Less-Than-Satisfactory Compromise

Marriage counselors, psychologists, and psychiatrists regularly deal with men and women who are barely coping with stale and dull marriages. Often these boring relationships lead these individuals to look outside the relationship for emotional and sexual satisfaction.

Some people get married to partners who provide much less in the relationship than is expected of them. The couple end up being housemates instead of soulmates. I call this marital situation the less-than-satisfactory compromise (LTSC). The less-than-satisfactory compromise may also be the result of a once exciting marriage having gone stale. The LTSC marriage is characterized by one or more of the following:

* One of the marriage partners doesn't love the other
* Both marriage partners don't love each other
* One or both of the partners feel empty and substantially unhappy

Your Singles Advantage

* No disagreements over which religion to follow
* Don't have to justify how you spend money

A less-than-satisfactory compromise is accepted for varying reasons. LTSC marriages occur because people are programmed that being married is natural and being single is unnatural. Some people marry to satisfy relatives and friends. Having somebody is better than having nobody is the philosophy that influences LTSC relationships. A LTSC marriage may also be the result of a shot-gun wedding where there was societal and parental pressure to marry; the couple may have felt that marrying was the right thing to do rather than remaining single.

Both men and women may also marry someone they don't love because they want to have children. This could be for the enjoyment of children, or to carry on the family name. Because no satisfactory partner is available to fall in love with, they end up marrying someone who is available.

Some marry into the less-than-satisfactory compromise because they have low self-esteem, and don't want to be regarded as someone unable to marry. "The belief that those who are part of a couple are more valued than those who are not" and "the need to lessen feelings of low self-esteem" are two negative reasons for marriage talked about by psychologist Michael Broder in *"The Art Of Living Single."* Both men and women accept the LTSC marriage because they want to be cared for by someone. Some people settle for the LTSC marriage because they want to feel safe. The LTSC marriage is a hoax, and can be self-destructive. Instead of safety and security, the LTSC marriage guarantees captivity of one form or another. The reality is the longer one stays in a boring compromise, the more difficult it is to let go in the future.

The problem with the less-than-satisfactory compromise is this kind of marriage may keep the negative things away, but it will also keep the good things away. A LTSC marriage ends up representing limitations rather than exciting possibilities. In a LTSC marriage, you end up saying it could be a lot worse; at the same time you disguise the fact that it could be a lot better. You forfeit the possibility of the authentically good marriage which would make your life so much more enjoyable and satisfying. In fact, being single is probably a lot more enjoyable and satisfying than a less-than-satisfactory marriage.

> *"In olden times sacrifices were made at the altar - a practice which is still continued."*
>
> - Helen Rowland

Marital Losers Or Marital Winners?

Some people keep trying at the game of marriage regardless of how many times they have divorced in the past. Psychiatrists Michael Liebowitz and Donald Klein of the New York State Psychiatrist Institute called people who crave a relationship "attraction junkies." These lovesick people regularly choose unsuitable partners; this leads to breakups and rejection. Some marriages don't last very long as the following three examples indicate:

Three Short Celebrity Marriages

* Jean Arthur and Julian Anker were married for one day.
* Patty Duke and William Tell were married for 13 days.
* George Brent and Constance Worth lasted 35 days.

One reason for marriage breakups may be that certain individuals are continually attracted to, or appeal to, members of the opposite sex who will do them absolutely no good. There are over 3,600,000 Americans who have married three or more times. Some people never learn according to Virginia sociologist Steven Nock. He states certain people tend to make questionable choices for marriage partners, which helps explain the high divorce rate for remarriages. Some mistakes he cites are:

> *"Why does a woman work ten years to change a man's habits and then complain that he's not the man she married?"*
>
> - Barbra Streisand

* Marrying a person without a job
* Marrying someone from a different religion
* Marrying someone with a substantially different amount of education

> *"I'd like to get married because I like the idea of a man required by law to sleep with me every night."*
>
> *- Carrie Snow*

Although divorce rates in the U.S. used to be higher when partners came from significantly different ethnic, religious, and socioeconomic backgrounds, sociologist Martin Whyte disputes that this is the case today. He found that these factors are rather insignificant. Instead, he contends significant differences in personality, values, interests, leisure activities, and friends are more responsible for the instability of marriages. Whyte also found that marrying at a younger age increases the risk of divorce. Divorce typically happens in the fourth year of marriage, with the risk of divorce subsiding as the number of years of marriage increases. The reasons people give for their divorces are many; here are some of the more common ones:

Reasons Why Couples Divorce

* Infidelity by partner
* Boredom
* Physical and mental abuse
* Jealousy
* Dishonest partner
* Found out partner is gay
* Partner has become an alcoholic or drug addict
* Partner wants too much or too little sex
* Partner watches too much TV
* Lack of communication
* Too many quarrels and fights
* Financial problems
* Infertility by partner
* Insensitivity

It should be noted that when people separate and divorce, they aren't necessarily giving up on marriage. They are just giving up on a particular marriage. Keep in mind that along with the famous people listed below, there are almost 4,000,000 people in the U.S. who have been married three or more times.

Some Of The Stars Who Married More Than Once

* Mickey Rooney was married eight times.
* Elizabeth Taylor was married eight times (twice to Richard Burton).
* Lana Turner was married eight times.
* Jennifer O'Neill was married seven times.

The above high-profile people by no means come close to the record for the most marriages in the United States. The Guinness Book of Records lists Linda Essex of Indiana as having the greatest number of monogamous marriages by a woman. She started marrying in 1957 and has now been married 22 times. The male record is held by a former Baptist Minister from California. Glynn (Scotty) Wolfe started marrying in 1927 and has been married 27 times. Although he isn't sure about the exact number, he believes he fathered 41 children.

Steven Nock has suggested the term "marital losers" for people who repeatedly make bad marital mistakes. Let's be fair here. Is Steven Nock on track? Certainly, there are over 3,600,000 Americans who have married three or more times. However, there are two ways of looking at these people: On one hand, these people may be considered, at the minimum, three-time losers. Because only lifelong marriage is considered a success in North America by many people, they associate divorce with failure.

"Guess what? Today I am getting a new set of golf clubs for my husband"

"That sounds like a real good trade."

On the other hand, some people look at divorce with a different point of view. Just because someone is married for the fourth time doesn't mean that he or she has already made three mistakes, and is potentially in the middle of the fourth. This person may feel that he or she has married four times and all four marriages were successful. Why does only a lifelong marriage have to be considered a success? A marriage terminated after four years can be considered a success if both partners were extremely happy for three years before running into a major problem. This marriage can be considered a greater success than one which lasted for 40 years, but both of the partners were unhappy and unfulfilled for 40 years.

> *"Marriage is the miracle that transforms a kiss from a pleasure to a duty."*
>
> *- Helen Rowland*

What To Do When The Wheels Fall Off

Many marriages run out of steam for one reason or another. At first, the partners couldn't wait to spend time in the same house and bed together. However, after several years - sometimes after even a month - the wheels fall off certain marriages. The partners have 1,000 reasons why their marriage was a bad idea, and shouldn't have happened in the first place.

Some couples grow together over the years, but others grow apart. When people grow apart, an unsatisfying marriage can be a lot more miserable than living alone. Marriage isn't a cure for loneliness or low self-esteem. Many couples living together side by side are like two railroad tracks that run in the same direction, but never touch. Marriages like this can actually influence people to be lonelier, and have lower self-esteem than they would have if they were single. Many people continue to stay in relationships for years when there is no longer any satisfaction. Here are the reasons people give for staying in unfulfilled marriages, which are at best dull and unsatisfactory compromises:

Why People Stay In Unhappy Marriages

* My parents would be upset and lose respect for me
* I am afraid of being alone
* I couldn't survive by myself
* What will my friends say?
* Everyone says that he's such a good catch

* I probably couldn't find someone else
* I would have less money
* Maybe he/she will change for the better with time
* It would hurt the children
* I would have to say that I am a failure

Some psychologists say the above reasons for staying in a relationship are unreasonable if there is no joy left. They advocate that the partners separate. However; before people decide to separate or divorce, they should read Michele Weiner-Davis's book *"Divorce Busting."* Weiner-Davis claims that most marriages can be saved if even just one partner wants it saved. She further claims that these marriages can be saved without the involvement of a therapist. Weiner-Davis believes that romance can be rekindled in most marriages, and creativity and spontaneity will go a long way to saving a marriage.

Your Singles Advantage

* **One less Christmas and Birthday gift to select and buy**
* **Don't have any worries about breaking up**

Singlehood may be the only option for some unhappy relationships. Note that I don't want to oversell singlehood. Unhappily married people can have the same myths about how divorce and singlehood will bring them happiness as they once had about how marriage will bring them happiness. The positives of singlehood are freedom, adventure, and mobility. Of course, there is the other side of single life - the negatives. To some individuals, single life can appear to be more exciting than it is in reality. Often, dissatisfied married people over-romanticize the single life.

Single life isn't Nirvana and shouldn't be considered by all dissatisfied married people as a key to total happiness. To someone who is used to marriage, becoming single again can take a lot of energy and cause a great deal of anxiety. With a divorce, things may become worse, before they become better.

In certain relationships, the situation is hopeless. The relationship is so bad that it can't be improved to a satisfactory state. Many psychologists say that in cases like this, no relationship is preferable to a really bad one. Thinking that having any marriage partner is better than no partner at all will undermine one's chances for a meaningful relationship with someone else. Staying in a bad relationship until one finds a better one generally won't work. This may keep the individual in the bad relationship forever.

> *"Bachelors know more about women than married men. If they didn't they'd be married too."*
>
> *- H. L. Mencken*

For some people, after having put a lot of energy and time into a marriage that isn't working, leaving the unhappy marriage may be the only way to happiness and self-respect. It takes a great deal of courage. Initially, changing one's marital status can be difficult and traumatic. In the long run, it may be the best thing to do. Singlehood may be the best answer.

To Marry Or To Remain Single? - You May Regret It Either Way

The issue of whether singles or married people are happier is certainly controversial. This interesting issue has probably been around for some time. *The People's Almanac* lists a book published in 1895 with the title *"How To Be Happy Though Married."* Certain studies indicate that singles aren't as happy as married people; other studies contradict this conclusion. Contrary to generally accepted, but erroneous beliefs, single people without a marital-type relationship can be just as happy in life as someone who is involved in an intimate relationship. Often, lonely people look to relationships to cure their loneliness. This seldom works - in many cases marriages actually add to people's loneliness.

> *"If we only wanted to be happy, it would be easy; but we want to be happier than most people, and that is almost always difficult, since we think them happier than they are."*
>
> *- Baron de Montesquieu*

Research at Ohio State University concludes it is a myth that loneliness is the result of living alone. A marriage certificate isn't essential for a fulfilled life. Single people have more friends than do people in

56

relationships, and well-adjusted singles are less troubled by headaches, anger, and irritability. Another research study confirms these findings. In interviewing never-married people between 58 and 94, two University of Guelph researchers, Joan Norris and Anne Martin Mathews, found the majority of singles are satisfied with their lives. People who stay single are known to develop strong friendships and have good jobs.

The *Vancouver Sun* in October, 1992 reported an interesting study conducted by Professor James White of the University of BC. White was quite skeptical when he read an article about an American researcher, who had concluded that marriage enhances health. White - himself married, healthy, and happy - was wondering if the American researcher missed the possibility that healthy single people were the ones who were getting married. This would result in healthy married people.

Your Singles Advantage

- **You don't have to remember an anniversary date**
- **Dating can be exciting and lots of fun**

When he started his own study, White was expecting to find that married people were healthier because they were the ones getting married. He found - much to his surprise - that singles were healthier. Single never-married females showed much greater health; however, single never-married men were also healthier in general than were married people. White discovered that never-married singles had happier and healthier scores in three of four categories that he used.

White noted that family life can be very stressful, especially for couples with small children and dual careers. Some of the most serious violence in our society occurs in the confines of family and marriage. Marriage seems to be getting more problem prone and stressful as the rate of change in the world keeps increasing. Marriage is supposed to offer

> *"Married men live longer than single men, but they suffer a slow, tortured death."*
>
> *- Larry Reeb*

Your Singles Advantage

- **No excessive demands are made for intimacy**
- **You can stay on the phone for as long as you want**

security; unfortunately, to many, it offers captivity. Married life isn't the normal and healthy route that it is made out to be. On the other hand, single life isn't as stigmatized as it once was. Professor White stated: "The advantages that married life used to have are diminishing and the disadvantages that single life used to have are diminishing so that the two are more similar."

I have cited these studies only to challenge the falsehoods that I hear about how all studies indicate married people, especially men, are the happiest and healthiest. Married men are certainly happier than recently divorced men, but recently divorced men aren't representative of well-adjusted singles. Many never-married singles are very happy with their situation in life, and don't consider themselves inferior to married people.

In the final analysis, these studies are totally irrelevant. True happiness is finding contentment within oneself. All the possessions in the world aren't going to bring anyone the happiness that some people with virtually no possessions experience from within. Similarly, the greatest marriage partner in the world won't make many people as happy as some single people. Your happiness depends on you and only you. It is your choice. You may be a bit happier in a wonderful marriage; however, you can be very happy being single. What it takes is some effort and a change in attitude.

Back to the issue of which is better - being married or being single? The story of the early Greek who had Socrates as a friend and confidant may resolve this issue quite nicely. This early Greek was perplexed about whether he should marry the woman he was madly in love with. He approached Socrates for advice on whether he should marry. Socrates in his wisdom replied: "You will regret it either way."

4. Some Important Purpose Is Calling You

Being On Purpose The Singles Way

One of the chief sources of happiness for successful single individuals is having a special purpose or personal mission. Some singles say that it is difficult to have an important purpose without a marriage partner sharing in their life's experiences. High-flying singles are passionate about their great purpose in life and don't need a relationship to make life worth living. Happy individuals with a personal mission say life is extraordinarily worth living - with or without an intimate relationship.

Although we all need love and companionship, we as creative people also need to be independent and autonomous. What adds greatly to our feelings of independence is having a unique purpose in life. This pursuit is normally separate from a relationship. Indeed, even individuals in the happiest of intimate relationships crave some great purpose in life, if they don't already have one.

> *"The deepest personal defeat suffered by human beings is constituted by the difference between what one was capable of becoming and what one has in fact become."*
>
> *- Ashley Montagu*

If you are having a hard time getting out of bed in the mornings, you haven't found your personal mission. Having an important purpose in life means being truly alive. In the mornings, you can't contain your high level of excitement and enthusiasm for the day ahead. You can't wait to get started whether it is raining, snowing, or sunny outside. Your personal mission is a calling in life which will be determined from within yourself. It comes from your soul; it is your essence and reason for being. Your personal mission is why you came into this world.

"I sometimes lie here meditating a bit about my greater purpose in life, but most of the time I just fantasize about getting laid."

Singles with a purpose have tenacity. The following great individuals have been admired and acknowledged in Western history: Isaac Newton, Mother Teresa, Blaise Pascal, Immanuel Kant, John Locke, and Henry David Thoreau. They were regarded as generally happy and satisfied in life. They also had something else in common: none of them ever married and most of them lived alone for the greater part of their lives. Their happiness in this world wasn't dependent upon their being attached. These individuals all had an important purpose in their lives and all made major contributions to society.

Anthony Storr in his book *"Solitude"* states: "There is a danger that love is being idealized as the only path to salvation." He further states: "One might argue that people who have no abiding interests other than their spouses and families are as limited intellectually as those who have neither spouse nor children may be emotionally." He thinks we have overemphasized love and intimacy, and not given enough attention to a strong purpose in life as a source of health and happiness. Storr concludes that individuals who are happiest in life are those who have struck a good balance between interpersonal relationships and their personal interests.

"Every individual has a place to fill in the world and is important in some respect whether he chooses to be so or not."

- Nathaniel Hawthorne

Happiness is finding your personal mission and responding to it with passion. It is important to find your personal mission if you are to live life with an overriding purpose. Most unhappy singles haven't found their ultimate purpose or personal mission. Many haven't found it because they haven't searched for it; some haven't found it because they don't know how to find it.

Your life will be much more rewarding if you put in the time and effort to find your personal mission, and then pursue it with passion. Neglecting your ultimate purpose or personal mission will cause you much dissatisfaction. Avoiding what you love may result in emotional turmoil and physical ailments. People who suppress their true interests and desires are most likely to get addicted to alcohol, drugs, work, or television in a futile attempt to ease the pain and dissatisfaction in their lives.

> *"It is not enough to be busy ... the question is: what are we busy about?"*
>
> *- Henry David Thoreau*

A personal mission is on a higher level than a goal. A goal, such as to become general manager of your organization, leaves you nothing to live for once you reach it. A personal mission, such as making the world a better place to live by having everyone reduce their pollution, is a higher calling. You can pursue this all your life.

Everyone can discover a primary purpose for living. Your personal mission can be expressed through your career or avocation, but it doesn't have to necessarily involve your work. It can also be expressed through volunteer work, a pastime, a hobby, or some other leisure activity. Your ultimate calling in life can be expressed through a combination of the various facets of your life, including your interests, your meaningful relationships, your work, and your leisure activities.

Vancouver nun Sister Beth Ann Dillon expresses her mission through basketball, her favorite sport. Needless to say, her personal mission is serving God by serving others. She lives a simple life free of material trappings, but one of joy. Basketball adds to her joy and helps her fulfill her mission. It seems Sister Dillon has loved basketball ever since she loved God. Through her volunteer work, she teaches basketball to girls in an elementary school. She believes playing basketball can bring people closer to God. In 1989, she met Pope John Paul in Chicago; she has also met Mother Teresa. Now with Vancouver about to have their own team, the Grizzlies, enter the National Basketball Association, she is excited about the possibility of meeting Michael Jordan.

> *"You have not done enough, you have never done enough, so long as it is still possible that you have something to contribute."*
>
> *- Dag Hammarskjold*

Are You Listening To Your Calling?

Your Singles Advantage

- **You can quit your job without having to explain why to a spouse**
- **No conflict with marriage partner over which hours you work**

Deepak Chopra in his book *"The Seven Spiritual Laws of Success"* gives seven laws for achieving success effortlessly. His seventh law is "Dharma." This means that everyone in life has unique talents and an important purpose. You won't lack zest for life if you discover your personal mission. Your essential nature will determine your purpose and what you truly want to accomplish in your life.

Your personal mission has nothing to do with: "Will I make a lot of money at this?" Having a personal mission or purpose means utilizing your unique talents in such a way that the conditions for humanity are enhanced. Your life is also enhanced because of the satisfaction and happiness you experience. While utilizing your talents in pursuing your mission, several by-products may result; one by-product may be making a lot of money.

A personal mission will be closely tied to your values and interests. It will also be determined by your strengths and weaknesses. A job which you take for the sole purpose of making money, and a leisure activity in which you participate to kill time, are not personal missions. Your personal mission is something that will make a difference in this world. If you have an overriding purpose in life, you know that humanity is benefiting from your efforts. A mission can be modest by other people's standards. For example, a friend's father is a school janitor whose mission is to create the cleanliest school possible for the students and teachers. Here are some other examples of personal missions:

* Make the world a better place to live by reducing pollution
* To raise money to help care for others in need
* To help children develop a special talent or skill such as playing a piano

* To write entertaining children books which help young boys and girls discover the wonder of the world

* To give foreign travelers the best possible tour of the Rocky Mountains

* To create a committed relationship and keep it exciting and energizing

Your personal mission will intimately connect you to who you are and to the world around you. Taking the time to answer the following questions may help reveal a personal mission which you would like to pursue.

1. What are all your passions? Discovering what turns you on is the most important element for recognizing your personal mission. Your passions give you great enjoyment; you seem to have unlimited energy when pursuing your passions. Write down all the things you find enjoyable. Your list can include things as varied as fishing, horses, serving others, researching at the library, making people laugh, and traveling to other countries. Pay attention to the things that would get you out of bed an hour or two earlier than your usual time.

2. What are your strengths? Looking at your strengths says something about yourself and where you like to concentrate your energy. If you are artistic and able to go with the flow, you may want to create art or music or sculpture. Strengths normally support passions.

3. Who are your heroes? Spend some time thinking about your hero or heroes who would be good role models. Heroes can be people from the past or present you have admired, or even revered. They can be famous or obscure people who are doing something special or outstanding. If you were given the opportunity, which three role models would you choose to have dinner with? What have these people accomplished that you admire? Studying your heroes' qualities and actions will give you clues about your own aspirations.

> *"Every calling is great when greatly pursued."*
>
> *- Oliver Wendell Holmes, Jr.*

4. What do you want to discover or learn? It is important to look at what stimulates your curiosity. Which topic or area would you like to explore more? Think about the courses or seminars you

> *"A musician must make music, an artist must paint, a poet must write, if he is to be ultimately at peace with himself."*
>
> *- Abraham Maslow*

would select if a wealthy relative appeared out of nowhere, and offered to finance two years of study anywhere in the world.

Answering these questions may put you on the right track to discovering your personal mission. When you get in touch with your innermost desires, you are connecting with your personal mission. No one else but you can discover your ultimate purpose in life.

If You Do Boring Work All Day, You Will End Up Boring

If you look at truly happy singles caught up in life, you will notice they are caught up in their life's purpose; often their purpose is their work. This holds true for the single individual who has an overwhelming passion for his or her work. Singlehood is a time to get established in work that is challenging and satisfying, especially if you have no children or other dependents. Is your work working for you? If it is, your work is your passion and constitutes part of your important purpose in life. Your important purpose will be manifested through your avocation when you are using your talents and creativity to make a difference in this world. If you are passionate about your work, you can be much happier than an attached person in an unfulfilled marriage and a boring, dead-end job.

If your job is primarily composed of tasks that you consider extremely boring, you should consider leaving. Bob Black in his essay *"Abolish Work: Workers Of The World, Relax"* offers some important food for thought. He states: "You are what you do. If you do boring, stupid, monotonous work, chances are you'll end up boring, stupid and monotonous."

> *"I had a boring office job. I cleaned the windows in the envelopes."*
>
> *- Rita Rudner*

If you are stuck in your career, leaving a less-than-mediocre job won't be easy. You may need the money and not have time to look for another job. However, if you have some opportunity to leave a boring and dehumanizing job, you must do it now for your long-term health and happiness. Making too many compromises to your lifestyle for the sake of your job makes for a miserable you.

Here is the content of a letter I received from Linda W., a single woman from Toronto, who decided to quit her secure job with the Ontario government and move to the interior of British Columbia:

Ernie, Ernie, Ernie

Just finished reading "The Joy Of Not Working" and I love it! You gave me the little boost that I needed with regards to pulling up stakes and heading to B.C.

I'm a part-time writer, public speaker, spiritual to the core and I have decided to head for the mountains of B.C. (even though there is a recession/depression), say to hell with the b.s. of a government office, good-bye concrete city and I am out of here.

You gave me that little something that said "go for it kid, you are not a fool to find peace of mind."

Yours truly,

Linda W.

> *"A working girl is one who quit her job to get married."*
>
> *- E.J. Kiefer*

Note that Linda W. didn't use any of these excuses: "there is a recession," "I can't leave a secure government job," or "I don't have the education for starting in a new field." She listened to her inner voice, which told her it was time to go. I am sure that she experienced at least some fear. She handled the fear by confronting it. She knew that she had to take risks if she was to experience some adventure and live life to the fullest.

Somewhere along the way, you may have had a sense of what you really would love to do. Instead, you chose a career or job considerably different from what could have been your passion. Over the years, you may have repressed this dream of a career with a higher purpose, because you concluded it was an unattainable fantasy. Now is the time to explore your dreams and wildest fantasies to give you some clues as to what you should be pursuing for a career.

When you are doing what you want to do, the things you enjoy, and the things you are good at, life becomes much easier. There are at least four reasons for this: First, you get satisfaction in life.

Second, you get to be very good at what you do. Third, money comes easier. Fourth, you feel good about how you earned your money.

Going For The Real Thing In Career Success

Sigmund Freud said work and love are the two keys to living happily as an individual. If this is the case, why are so many people, who are working and married, unhappy even if they have decent marriages? The problem is they haven't attained career success.

Exercise: Which of these are essential for career success?

- Superior intelligence
- Special skills
- Working in fields such as law, medicine, or architecture
- Luck
- Knowing the right people
- A high level of formal education
- Hard work

It may come as a surprise to you, but not one of the above items is essential for career success. Millions of well-educated, richly skilled, and highly intelligent people haven't attained career success. At the same time, North America is full of hard working people putting in ten to fourteen-hour days who also haven't attained career success. An accountant making $30,000 a year in a dead-end job is experiencing career failure; so is a lawyer making $150,000 a year if she dislikes her profession.

"It is your work in life that is the ultimate seduction."

- Pablo Picasso

What I mean by career success is getting satisfaction and enjoyment out of one's chosen work. Studies indicate that over 80 percent of people don't like what they are doing for a living. Almost 25 percent of people feel they are in "dumb" jobs for which they are overqualified. Incidentally, just in case you disagree with me and define getting rich as career success, millions of well-educated, richly skilled, and highly intelligent people, who work hard all their lives, wind up broke in retirement.

My premise is that career success can only be attained if you work at a job which is such a turn-on that you would work at it for free, just to experience the satisfaction from doing it. To attain job satisfaction, you need to be passionate about your work. Matthew Fox, author of *"Reinvention of Work,"* states:

> *"When you see what some girls marry, you realize how they must hate to work for a living."*
>
> - Helen Rowland

"Work touches your heart and it has to touch other people's hearts. If there's one question I would ask to awaken us to spiritual work, it would be: 'How does your work touch the joy in you and what joy does your work bring out in others?'"

When your work is your passion, there is no distinction between work and play. In the old concept of work, you won't have to "work" another day in your life. But, I can't decide for you what your passion is; you have to do this yourself.

The reason so many people from the baby-boom generation are suffering from a mid-life crisis is they never pursued a job or career which is their passion. During the 1980s, most of these people pursued careers or jobs which paid the most money, so they could live the yuppie lifestyle of excess materialism. They may have achieved career success as they defined the term. They got to the top of the corporate ladder and attained their material possessions. The problem is their marriages may be in shambles, their children are all messed up, and they themselves are suffering from excessive stress and dissatisfaction.

What is essential for their career success is working at something they enjoy; they must be serving others in a positive way. An enriched life won't be available to those dissatisfied workers who switch jobs, unless they find a job which coincides with, or supports, their personal mission. Also more important than economic factors in job selection should be the issue of lifestyle or quality of life. A balance between work and

Your Singles Advantage

- **Can nap without having to justify it to anyone**
- **You have more sources of stimulation**

personal life is much more important than acquiring more money and material possessions than everyone else.

> *"There is something wrong with my eyesight. I can't see going to work."*
>
> *- Teddy Bergeron*

The biggest obstacle to people achieving career success is a lack of self-esteem. Most people are held captive by programming about what success means to parents and society. Many people unhappy in their careers are working at unsuitable jobs because they are trying to fulfill someone else's dream, instead of their own. On the extreme, many employees are so miserable that they are suffering from ongoing job-related stress.

If you have a mediocre job, more money isn't the answer. The idea, "If I was paid more in my job, then I would be happier with what I do," is a myth. The opposite is often true. If you were happier with what you do, you would make more money. If your job has little connection with your values and real interests, you will feel dissatisfied regardless of how much money you make.

You should try to find work that enriches your body and mind. You want to be rewarded for your work with praise, raises, promotions, and room for growth. Your job should give you some level of control and flexibility. Finding creative employment should be your goal. Do what you like or what you are. If you are artistic or a good leader, try to put these talents to use in your career. You have to be somewhat realistic. It's a case of being creative and doing the most with what you have.

Deepak Chopra in his book *"The Seven Spiritual Laws of Success"* suggests that career success can be achieved effortlessly. His fourth law is The Law Of Least Effort. The American core value that hard work and goal orientation are necessary for career success is wrong according to Chopra. You can accomplish more by doing less. The key is avoiding the goal of attaining power and control of others. Also, avoid expending energy in seeking approval from others. The easiest path to prosperity is doing what you enjoy and forgetting about what other people think of you. When you enjoy your work, little effort is required to attain satisfaction. This represents true career success.

> *"All paid jobs absorb and degrade the mind."*
>
> *- Aristotle*

When choosing a career related to your purpose or mission, you need to be aware of your aspirations. Listen to your inner voice, and not to what others tell you to do or be. If your work is your passion, you will be highly motivated to achieve great things, and your chances for monetary success will be enhanced.

Workplaces can be exciting, challenging, active, stimulating, and innovative. They can also be dull, routine, frustrating, dejecting, and boring. You must choose your employer wisely. Make sure that your job is enjoyable and satisfying, and that you have room to grow and learn. You want to be valued for your new ideas, your positive energy, and your ability to be productive.

The key to a satisfying job is to utilize your special talents at something you love. Ron Smotherman in his book "*Winning Through Enlightenment*" stated: "Satisfaction is for a very select group of people: those who are willing to be satisfied. There aren't many around." Do you want to be in the select group of people who are satisfied in their work? If the answer is yes, then you have to keep asking yourself the important questions mentioned earlier: What are you good at? What are your talents? How about your strengths and weaknesses? Which would you like to use and improve in a career? Would you ever do a certain type of work for free just for the enjoyment? Keep asking yourself these questions every day for the next year if you have to. The answers may eventually lead you into work that you can be passionate about.

The Joy Of Not Working Nine To Five

You must not feel totally imprisoned at work. Are you sick of the rat race, dejected by the win-at-all-costs mentality, and tired of being tired? If you are, get out while the getting is good, and while you still have time to pursue something different which will turn you on, and reward you with personal growth. Leaving a less-than-satisfactory job won't be easy. Breaking up is always hard to do, especially if the money is good. What good is financial success if you are miserable, bored, and empty? Do you want to look back in your life, and say you had all the material comforts which you didn't get to enjoy?

> "They all attain perfection when they find joy in their work."
>
> - Bhagavad Gita

If you have recently been downsized, or are about to be, this may be a blessing in disguise. You may be able to turn a negative situation into a positive one. Now may be the time to challenge your need for security and unwillingness to take a risk. Searching for a regular job may appear to be the safe way out, but you may be selling yourself short. This may be the opportune time to pursue something which is creative and fulfilling. Sure, there is the fear of the unknown, but finding another regular job carries the risk that you may be downsized again in six months or a year. You may attain much more security by pursuing a career with your personal mission in mind. If you get established in a business of your own, you won't ever have to consider working for anyone else again.

As a writer and professional speaker, I can vouch for the advantages of not working for someone else. Having paid the price of searching and discovering what I want to do, I am doing what I enjoy most on my terms. There is no life like it - what a great way to make a living! Why work for any one of millions of bosses when I can work for my favorite boss - ME? As mentioned before, I only ask that I work four hours a day. I also give myself permission to avoid working in any month that doesn't have an "r" in it. By working less, I may not make a lot of money compared to what I could make working twelve hours a day. However, it's all relative. My income looks really good to the employees who work at the local car wash.

> *"When one has no particular talent for anything, one takes to the pen."*
>
> *- Honore de Balzac*

Breaking away from conventional employment by working for yourself in your own business, or as a contract employee, gives you more opportunity to attain job satisfaction. One advantage is that you don't have someone telling you what to do. You have control over your workplace and flexibility in when and how you work.

On one of my promotional trips for *"The Joy Of Not Working,"* I met Ben Kerr during an open-line radio interview on CFRB-AM in Toronto. Kerr telephoned to say that he was now a busker at the intersection of Yonge and Bloor. He mentioned that he had written a song called *"I Don't Want To Be The Richest Man In The Graveyard."* I offered to meet him at Yonge and Bloor the next day, and give him a copy of my book if he sang me the song.

When I first met Ben Kerr, the thing I noticed is that he is an extremely happy man. While he sings his songs throughout the afternoon, people from all walks of life continually say hello to him and give him money. Over the years, Ben has been offered several jobs, but he is like me - he isn't interested in working for someone else. He is having too much fun. He gets more satisfaction and adulation singing at Yonge and Bloor than 90 percent of people get from their work. Inspired by my book, Ben has written a song called *"The Joy Of Not Working Nine To Five."* Here are the words:

> *"Music is my mistress and she plays second fiddle to no one."*
>
> *- Duke Ellington*

The Joy Of Not Working Nine To Five

I know the joy of not working nine to five
Singing every day at Yonge and Bloor
Strumming my old 5-string guitar
It's the joy of not working and that's for sure

People say that I'm a lucky guy
And they wish that they could be like me
To know the joy of not working from nine to five
To be foot-loose and fancy free

But they'll never loose the treadmill that they're on
And it's sad to see dejection in their eyes
The joy of not working could be there
But they're just too afraid to try

Ernie J. Zelinski wrote a book
***The Joy Of Not Working* is its name**
'Cause Ernie is a fellow just like me
And the joy of not working is his game

I know the joy of not working nine to five
Singing every day at Yonge and Bloor
Strumming my old 5-string guitar
It's the joy of not working and that's for sure

Strumming my old 5-string guitar at Yonge & Bloor
It's the joy of not working and that's for sure
The joy of not working and that's for sure

© 1994 by Ben Kerr

Developing mental self-sufficiency will go a long way in this day and age. Sources of support, such as governments, employers, and non-profit organizations, can't be relied on as much as they were in the past. Employment opportunities are disappearing rapidly. Self-sufficiency will help you deal with any job loss. You will know that you are still a meaningful and valuable individual who has a lot to offer. The day you become mentally self-sufficient will be the day your self-esteem and well-being are elevated to new heights.

A Purpose For The Unemployed

It is important that you have some purpose in life, whether you are working or unemployed. If your personal mission is impossible to pursue through your work, then find a purpose which you can serve outside work. If you are disadvantaged, make your purpose to live life to the fullest and enjoy it more than people who aren't disadvantaged.

Having a purpose can be a matter of life or death. People without purpose don't seem to live as long as those with purpose. Much of the literature on retirement quotes statistics indicating that people without purpose in retirement aren't known for breaking records for longevity. Many people, who don't create a new purpose outside of work, die of boredom a year or two after retiring.

One way many seniors and younger individuals can create a purpose is by volunteering for an organization which is pursuing something dear to them. Many volunteers profess that there is nothing more satisfying than experiencing the higher calling of serving others. Great personal rewards can be realized from donating time to others who truly need the help.

Most major cities have an association which directs prospective volunteers to appropriate charities and non-profit associations. Your volunteer work can take many forms, such as working at a charity-sponsored bingo, assisting the handicapped or the mentally ill, helping the homeless by working in a soup kitchen, building new low-income housing, renovating run-down apartments, becoming involved in a local theatre production, playing music for a non-profit choir or

"We work not only to produce but to give value to time."

- Eugene Delacroix

orchestra, raising funds for a charity, or assisting victims of abuse in a crisis center.

Sharing your energy and talents with others may be a creative way to overcome periods of loneliness and boredom. By helping others in need solve their problems, you may be solving one or two of your own. You may even end up meeting someone special, and disappearing into the sunset with him or her.

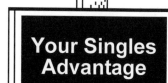

Your Singles Advantage

- **You can put more time into a career**
- **No spouse is envious of your career accomplishments**

Life Without Purpose Is Life Without Direction

In his book *"The Master Game,"* D.S. DeRopp stated: "Seek above all for a game worth playing. Such is the oracle to modern man. Having found the game, play it with intensity, play as if your life and sanity depend on it. (They do depend on it.)"

Contributing to the world in a meaningful way helps us earn self-respect and the respect of others. The longing for meaning and purpose in our lives is normal. A sense of usefulness is essential for your satisfaction in life, especially as you grow older. Be clear about who you are and what you want out of life. You should have a reason to get up in the morning. When you have a true purpose or personal mission, you have a sense that you are making a difference in the lives of others.

No one's life needs to lack purpose. You have to discover or create your own purpose if you want to feel that you are making a real difference in this world. You have to tap your creativity to discover your purpose.

Not having discovered your personal life mission at 30 or 40 years of age doesn't mean you won't find it. Many people haven't discovered what they really wanted to do until mid-life or later. Regardless of how old you are, it is never too late to reinvent yourself, discover your mission, and pursue it

> *"I never thought of achievement. I just did what came along for me to do - the thing that gave me the most pleasure."*
>
> *- Eleanor Roosevelt*

> *"The purpose of life is not to be happy. It is to be useful, to be honorable, to be compassionate, to have it make some difference that you have lived and lived well."*
>
> *- Ralph Waldo Emerson*

with vigor. If you need an education to arrive at that career that will coincide with your mission, then get it. An excuse that arises is: "But I am 49 and I will be 53 when I get there." In four years, you are going to be 53 anyway. If you don't do what you have to, you will be 53 and just as dissatisfied, or possibly more dissatisfied, than you are today. Your personal mission will surface if you are ready for it. Here are three examples of people involved in a personal mission at a later age:

* Red Skelton at 81 shows much more zest for life than most people in their twenties and thirties. Why? He has a personal mission which is to entertain people and make them happy. Skelton gets only three hours of sleep because he goes to bed at 2:30 AM and rises at 5:30 AM. He spends his time writing stories, composing music, and painting. As an entertainer, he still averages 75 live performances a year.

* Martin Miller of Indiana at 97 was working full-time lobbying for the rights of senior citizens.

* Mary Baker Eddy was 87 when she followed her personal mission - starting a new newspaper with a religious influence. She called it the *Christian Science Monitor.*

You must not stop pursuing goals just to please or compete with others. The key is to create a purpose which you are passionate about. If you can establish some ultimate mission in your life, you will have a fiery driving force to keep your life exciting and interesting. This will ensure you are constantly growing and learning.

Discovering your purpose is the cornerstone for using your personal creativity. The biggest challenge will be looking within, discovering your purpose, and living out that purpose. Your life should never be without purpose. Your personal mission should relate to your essence and your dreams. Being on purpose means each task, act, and situation will be worthy of your total attention. Discovering your personal mission will give you a direction in life which is truly your own.

5. Be Creative Or Else!

You Can Be More Creative Than Picasso Or Van Gogh

While you are engaged in your personal mission, your creativity will be your resource for overcoming barriers such as society's norms, inadequate finances, objections of relatives, not enough skills, or limited time because of your children's needs. Creativity is the ultimate gift available to singles dealing with the challenge of living happily. Single's blues can strike anytime. If anything will lead you out of boredom and loneliness, your imagination will. Highly creative individuals find that their most significant accomplishments occur when they are alone. New insights and discoveries usually don't involve another person with whom one has an intimate or meaningful relationship.

> "Everyone is a genius at least once a year; a real genius has his original ideas closer together."
>
> - C.C. Lichtenberg

"But, I'm not creative" you say. Nonsense! You were born creative as was every human being. You have to rediscover your creativity and start using it to your advantage. So there you go! You have long suspected that you are a latent genius, but you haven't had the courage to share your suspicions with anyone. Now you can.

You can use your imagination to enhance your life in many ways. If you are a single parent, being more creative will help you manage your personal affairs, establish support networks, make ends meet on a low income, care for your children, and work at a full-time job (or two part-time ones) to support your household. Establishing a satisfying lifestyle, despite many obstacles, will prove you are much more creative than Picasso, Van Gogh, and Renoir ever were.

Using your imagination will make you a much happier and more satisfied single. Being creative means utilizing new ways of thinking; it also means looking at things in a fresh way. New approaches are possible for just about anything. Abraham Maslow stated that a truly good soup can be as creative as a great painting or a marvelous symphony. New approaches are possible for music, painting, cooking, engineering, carpentry, accounting, law, economics, leisure, sports, and living single.

Dispelling Your Romantic Notions About Creativity

If you still aren't convinced that you are a creative genius, forget whatever romantic notions you have about creativity - your romantic notions should be focused on more important things like finding a marriage partner, if that is what you want. Creativity isn't a gift from God given only to certain artists and musicians. Creativity also isn't dependent upon a lot of suffering, nor is it associated with a touch of madness. Some people think that one or more of the following factors are essential for anyone to be creative:

- Having rare artistic talent
- Having had parents who encouraged creativity
- Having an education in the fine arts
- Being right rather than left brained
- Having a high IQ
- Early independence as a child

> *"Every child is an artist. The problem is how to remain an artist once he grows up."*
>
> *- Pablo Picasso*

Creativity is often thought to be a matter of special skill, ability, knowledge, or effort. In fact, not one of the above factors is essential for creative success. If you take a hard look at creative people, they are simply "being" creative. They are expressing excellence and creativity, because they made the choice. Creative people don't believe they need exceptional talent to be creative.

Many people believe that the sequence from "HAVE" to "DO" to "BE" represents the road to creativity. Their belief is that a person must first "HAVE" what creative people have: inherited intelligence, artistic talent, right-brain tilt, and a host of other things. Then the person will "DO" what creative people do. Finally, the person will "BE" creative. This belief is false. There is no truth to the belief that creative people have special talent which enables them to be creative, and non-creative people don't have this talent. Researchers have confirmed that non-creative people have all the talent necessary to be creative.

I meet many people who want to be writers. More than "being" a writer, which takes effort and commitment, most of these people want all the trappings that accompany being a well-known writer. They want to have a bestselling book or two with their names on them, and have the fame and fortune that Danielle Steele and John Grisham have. People also aspire to being writers because they want to do the things well-known writers do, such as participate at writers conferences and appear on radio and television talk shows.

"Being" a writer doesn't happen after first having a bestselling book and appearing on talk shows to promote it. Aspiring writers can't ever do what writers do, and have what writers have, unless they first choose to "be" writers. Being a writer doesn't happen after the doing and having. Being a writer first requires making the choice to "be" a writer, which leads to doing and having what writers do and have.

> *"Happiness lies in the joy of achievement and the thrill of creative effort."*
>
> *- Franklin Roosevelt*

Reversing the above stated sequence better represents the road to creativity. The right order is from "BE" to "DO" to "HAVE." First, we must choose to "BE" creative. Then, we will "DO" the things that creative people do. What will follow naturally is we will "HAVE" the things that creative people have. The "HAVE" things for a writer include accomplishment, satisfaction, and happiness experienced from attempting and completing a challenging project.

This concept isn't something new. Taoism extols the importance of "BEING." Classic Chinese Taoist philosophy was first documented by Lao-tzu some 2500 years ago in his book *"Tao-te Ching."* Lao-tzu emphasizes that to be truly alive, you must first "BE." Once you have mastered the art of "BEING," then "DOING" and "HAVING" will flow naturally. "BEING" is an active state - a creative process that helps you change and grow as a person. So, "BE" creative or else!

An Artistic Day For Non-Artistic Individuals

One way to get in touch with yourself and the artist or creator within yourself is to have a planned Artistic or Creator's Day once a week. Call it whatever you want to call it. This is a special outing during which you celebrate your imagination along with your unique interests in the world. It doesn't matter whether you think that you lack artistic talent. This weekly routine of taking time for yourself will trigger creative talents that you haven't used for some time, or didn't know you had.

"Very few people do anything creative after the age of thirty-five. The reason is that very few people do anything creative before the age or thirty-five."

- Joel Hildebrand

On this day, once a week, for the next three or four months, you get to be alone to pursue something new you have always wanted to pursue, or have previously enjoyed doing but have set aside. It is important that you be alone when you participate in this activity. You don't want to be concerned about criticism from others. This is also a time to enjoy being alone.

If you haven't been using your God-given creative ability which you used as a child, rediscovering your creativity will enhance your life. Writing is one way to express your creativity. It can be a novel or a daily journal in which you write your life story. If writing isn't for you, then try wood carving or restoring an old car. The activity can be something truly artistic such as painting, sculpturing, or writing. It can also be an activity, such as photographing a series of pictures, which is considered less artistic by some "elitists." Start by listing fifteen things you like doing or have always wanted to pursue. Your list may include some of the following activities:

* Write a book
* Paint a series of pictures
* Critique ten movies
* Explore all the interesting sights in your area
* Write a number of songs
* Photograph all the species of birds in your area
* Visit a variety of restaurants to discover the diversity of available meals in your city

* Attend and critique a combination of symphony, opera, and live theatre performances
* Learn to play a musical instrument

Once you have developed your list, choose some interest to pursue with focus, purpose, and concentration. You must stick to this activity for at least twelve weeks. For twelve weeks or more, you get to be the artist or creator. The importance of this day is celebrating the process, and not the outcome. For example, if you have chosen to write a book, it doesn't matter if the book gets published. The process of your writing the book is important, because you are actually writing it, instead of just thinking about it.

> *"To paint a fine picture is far more important than to sell it."*
>
> *- Edward Alden Jewell*

Once you start writing the book or painting your pictures, you will start to discover your creativity. You will also get to appreciate being alone. Your Artist's or Creator's Day will connect you with your creativity, which you have always had, but suppressed. You will discover you are much more creative than you thought you were.

When you eventually finish the project, you will experience a great deal of satisfaction and self-confidence. Now, you can also celebrate the outcome. If you chose to write a book, you can now risk and show it to friends or relatives. If you chose to paint a series of pictures, so what if someone thinks that all of them look like the bottom of Lake Superior? Regardless of what they have to say, you will feel an incredible sense of accomplishment from completing your project. You will have seen creative qualities in yourself that you didn't see before. Taking the time to do something imaginative, and showing the commitment to take the time for yourself on a regular basis, will help you to develop more confidence and courage to live as a happy single.

The following letter, sent to me in February, 1995 from a man in Winnipeg, shows the power of rediscovering one's creativity:

Mr. Zelinski

Your book The Joy Of Not Working pinpointed many of the things that are wrong with our society, such as materialism and the crazy attitude we have towards work. But what impressed me the most was how you stressed that people should use their creativity and

79

imagination to get more out of life.

After reading the book I began to look at my life in a much different way. To my surprise I found a creative side of me that I never knew existed. I just spent the last year writing a book and I have never felt so good about accomplishing something. So good that I just had to write you. Throughout the writing, my motto has always been straight from page 131: "If your book is enjoyed by one person other than yourself, it is a success - anything over and above this is a bonus."

Respectively,

N.K.

Whether it is writing or learning to play a piano, a creative outlet will help you enjoy being alone and confirm your creativity. The major difference between creative people and non-creative people is creative people believe that they can be creative. They know that creativity can be learned. Imaginative people don't deny their abilities and potentials; they realize that they have to choose to be creative.

To Be More Creative, Forget What You Know

To be more creative, try setting aside your knowledge. You may have to challenge, and even forget, what you know. Knowledge is not creativity. Knowledge is about what you already know; creativity is about what you don't know, but intend to find out.

> *"Much knowledge is a curse."*
>
> *- Chuang-Tzu*

The distinction between creativity and knowledge is important. Stephen Leacock said: "Personally, I would sooner have written *'Alice in Wonderland'* than the whole *'Encyclopedia Britannica'*." Albert Einstein was emphasizing the same point when he said: "Imagination is much more important than knowledge." What Leacock and Einstein were saying is that imagination transcends knowledge.

Researchers have determined that emotional intelligence and creative ability are more important for real life success than accumulated knowledge and academic intelligence. Many academics and intellectuals parade their knowledge wherever they go, but they fall short when it comes to imagination. Since they focus too much on their knowledge, many academically bright people don't think creatively. They have self-destructive habits of mind and hold back from new challenges because they lack the necessary emotional smarts. Intellectuals spend a lot of time contemplating hypothetical and academic matters, but they fail to develop the creative abilities needed to deal with reality.

Isn't It Time To Give Your Mind An Overhaul?

Researchers have estimated every human brain has about one million, million or 1,000,000,000,000 braincells. Despite the many braincells at their disposal, many people use only a few. Researchers say people use only ten percent of their total brains. No wonder most of us aren't highly creative; we are wasting about 90 percent of our brains' potential. Indeed, approximately 95 percent of people are dissatisfied with their mental performance.

> *"If your mind is empty, it is always ready for anything; it is open to everything. In the beginner's mind there are many possibilities; in the expert's mind there are few."*
>
> *- From Zen, Beginner's Mind*

Being creative is being able to question why we do and think certain things. It is paying attention instead of being unconscious. We all do silly things on our own, or allow ourselves to be brain washed by society to do things which are, if not totally stupid, ridiculous at best.

We also don't stop to question why we are doing or thinking things that could be considered silly or suspect. Below are just a few things that people in society do without thinking about the merits, or how unproductive the results may be. In most of these examples, people doing these things certainly don't seem to have utilized more than 1,000 of their 1,000,000,000,000 braincells questioning why they are doing these things.

Signs Of Uncreative Thinking Or Questionable Things People Do

* People with MBA degrees who think that nearly everything that they learned in business courses is relevant to real life
* Healthy and able people who believe governments are responsible for them
* Single people who believe that there is someone who will come and rescue them from all their problems
* People who believe the only way to get rich is to win a lottery

* People who can't think of more than one way to make an egg stand on its end
* People who are addicted to the Shopping Channel
* Editors who get overly concerned about split infinitives
* People who can't think of at least one original rebus
* People who jog or walk in the middle of the street when the government has spent millions of dollars on sidewalks
* Advertising agencies which follow the latest industry trend
* People who spend days trying to think up new palindromes
* People who know what palindromes are
* People who believe Elvis is alive and God is dead
* People who have worked for 30 years and haven't been fired at least once in their careers
* People who get involved in chain letter schemes for money
* People who show everyone how different they are even though they are just copying the latest fad
* People making $50,000 a year who get caught shoplifting
* People who own more than 20 pairs of shoes
* Everyone who sees themselves in this list and gets mad at me
* Anyone who thinks of lists like this
* Anyone who takes this list seriously

> *"The great creative individual ... is capable of more wisdom and virtue than collective man ever can be."*
>
> *- John Stuart Mill*

In certain ways, creative thinking is nothing more than common sense. It is the ability to question things, and then take action accordingly. A doctorate degree or high intelligence level can't take the place of real-life experience combined with the power of imagination. Harry Gale took a little time to find this out. In early 1995, Gale was ousted from his position as executive director of MENSA in Britain. MENSA is an organization for people who have proven to have IQs representing something like the top two percent of the population. Apparently, Harry Gale finally saw the light as soon as he was sent down the road by this elitist organization. He set up a rival organization called Psicorp which recruits members from all walks of life. In an interview with *The Sunday Times Of London*, Gale stated: "Common sense is quite often more important than intelligence."

What Is Blocking Your Creativity?

As a society, we are so involved in trying to acquire knowledge, material goods, and marriage partners to help us through life that we forget that our natural creativity is the ultimate tool to help us deal with life. We as adults have allowed many blocks or barriers to stand in the way of our creativity. By the time we are in mid-adulthood, we have lost virtually all of the creativity which we had as children.

Business Week magazine some time ago reported that a 40-year-old adult is about two percent as creative as a child of five. What has happened to our creative abilities during those years in between childhood and adulthood? Obviously, we encounter many blocks or barriers to expressing our imagination in the world around us, if we have lost 98 percent of our creativity by the time we are 40 years old. There are four major blocks to our creativity:

> *"The jean! The jean is the destructor. It is a dictator! It is destroying creativity! The jean must be stopped!"*
>
> *- Pierre Cardin*

- Society
- Educational Institutions
- Organizations
- Ourselves

The biggest block to our creativity is ourselves since we are the ones who allow ourselves to be influenced by society, organizations, and educational institutions. We also erect many individual barriers which also rob us of the opportunity to use our imaginations. Fear of failure is one of the more effective robbers of our creativity. Right beside fear stand laziness and perception. All of these can interfere with our willingness to accept the challenge of undertaking new projects in our lives.

Seventeen Principles For Rediscovering Your Creativity

To rediscover and utilize your creativity, just start using the following seventeen principles of creativity which form the basis of my book *"The Joy Of Not Knowing It All."* These seventeen principles can be applied to personal matters as well as career and business affairs. When you start applying these creativity principles to your work and play, your life will change immensely regardless of your occupation or age.

Seventeen Principles Of Creativity

- Choose to be creative.
- Look for many solutions.
- Write your ideas down.
- Fully analyze your ideas.
- Define your goal.
- See problems as opportunities.
- Look for the obvious.
- Take risks.
- Dare to be different.
- Be unreasonable.
- Have fun and be foolish.
- Be spontaneous.
- Be in the now.
- Practice divergent thinking.
- Challenge rules and assumptions.
- Delay your decision.
- Be persistent.

The most important thing to remember is that if anyone is responsible for blocking your imagination, it is you. Despite all the barriers and influences affecting our creativity, researchers have concluded everyone is born with creative abilities, and everyone can rediscover these abilities. Whether you want to be more creative at writing, painting, dancing, finding a new route home, or meeting a new person, you don't require special talent. What is necessary is your willingness to be imaginative by using the above seventeen principles of creativity.

Creative minds always have been known to survive any kind of bad training."

- Anna Freud

What Is The Real Problem?

Using the above principles of creativity to solve your problems will enhance both your career and personal life. In applying these principles of creativity to any problem, I must stress the importance of first identifying the problem. You may think that your problem is your unhappiness, because you don't have a marriage partner, when your actual problem is you are unhappy due to a lack of self-esteem. Generating a lot of solutions for finding a marriage partner may result in your finding a partner, but your unhappiness will persist because you haven't solved the real problem of having low self-esteem. If you define the problem correctly as unhappiness due to lack of self-esteem, then your solutions will be more effective in solving the issue of unhappiness.

> *"A problem well stated is a problem half solved."*
>
> *- Charles F. Kettering*

Identifying the problem is crucial. Let me give you another example. At a conference at the Banff Springs Hotel for young adults involved with Junior Achievement, I was all set to make my keynote speech. The hotel sound technician wouldn't let me proceed due to the apparent feedback on the sound system. He asked me to turn off the "on" button on my clip-on cordless microphone, which I did. The sound persisted so he asked me to turn off the power supply, which I also did. Fifteen minutes after my speech was supposed to commence, the technician was going crazy still trying to figure out what was causing the feedback. Much to his astonishment, turning off the power for both the main sound system and the cordless microphone hadn't helped.

That is when I thought: "Have we identified the problem correctly?" I then walked to the back of the auditorium and there was the problem staring me in the face. Four high-school students were all rubbing the rim of their water glasses with their forefingers and creating the high-pitched noise you have undoubtedly heard before. This sounds similar to the feedback that comes from sound systems. Because we hadn't identified the problem correctly, we didn't stand a chance of coming up with an effective solution. We still could have been there trying to figure out what was causing the "feedback" problem if the problem hadn't been correctly identified.

So don't forget to spend a little time, or even a lot of time, just determining what your actual problem is. What is the use of generating a lot of brilliant solutions if you don't have a clue what the problem is?

Creating Opportunity Rather Than Waiting For It

Most of us are apt to look for one way to do most tasks. If this single way doesn't work well, we still stick with it and find someone or something to blame for the situation being unworkable. We don't look for new ways, although another way may be quicker, more efficient, or less costly. Being creative is being able to see or imagine a great deal of opportunity in life's problems. Creativity is having many options, that we wouldn't otherwise generate if we didn't look for them. Just spending a little more time looking can result in remarkable solutions as the following exercise indicates.

Assume the equation below is made with match sticks. Each line in the characters is one match stick. The equation is wrong the way it stands. Can you, by moving just one match stick, make the equation correct?

$$III - II = IV$$

One of the most important creativity principles is there are two or more solutions to virtually all of life's problems. If you thought of only one solution to the above exercise, you didn't put enough effort into solving it. Note that highly creative individuals will have no significant problem in thinking of at least seven solutions to this exercise. Many people will think of five or so; some will stop after only one or two. (Refer to page 94 for some of my solutions to this exercise.)

"It isn't that they can't see the solution. It is that they can't see the problem."

- G.K. Chesterton

If you stopped after one or two solutions to this exercise, do you also stop after one or two solutions to your everyday problems at work or play? You are missing out on many opportunities in your life if you are thinking of only one or two solutions, when there are many solutions, or in some cases, even an endless number.

The number of ways that you can use your

imagination to enhance your life while living single is unlimited as well. Some of the benefits you will get from making the effort to be more creative are increased self-esteem, personal growth, more enthusiasm for solving problems, increased confidence to deal with new challenges, and different perspectives toward work and personal life.

> *"Most people would sooner die than think: in fact, they do."*
>
> *- Bertrand Russell*

Seeing the opportunity in life extends beyond seeing the available and the obvious. What do we have to do to create many new solutions? It is essential we first let go of the old so we experience a state of nothingness. Opportunity is literally created from a state of nothingness. When we let go of old solutions and old ways of thinking, we have a clear slate from which we can create.

What A Difference Being Different Makes!

Society's norms often dictate how we act and the goals we pursue. We think that to feel good about ourselves, we must be liked by everyone, or at least as many people as possible. Indeed, just to belong to a group, we end up doing things which aren't in touch with our inner selves. This is when we lose sense of who we really are.

If you want to lead an anonymous life, then go ahead and be like everyone else - fit in and be part of the pack. Conforming to society, and thinking like the rest of the herd, is just another case of doing the easy thing for short-term comfort. There is nothing unique about you. The result is you get to fit in and be liked a little bit by everyone. However, in the long term, life is difficult because your self-respect suffers, and there is no satisfaction from having accomplished something significantly different.

There is no question that not conforming and not fitting in are often uncomfortable. You have to confront the discomfort of people jeering and criticizing you. The long-term payoff is you gain self-respect and satisfaction. Other highly motivated people will end up admiring and congratulating you for having the fortitude to stand apart from the boring crowd.

> *"All profoundly original art looks ugly at first."*
>
> *- Clement Greenberg*

Don't fit in just to be liked and accepted by the group. Insist on being an individual who has something unique to offer to anyone who likes individuals, and not clones. Going against the status quo and removing yourself from the herd give you a sense of who you really are.

Being different means not doing something even though everyone else is doing it. When someone suggests that you should do something because "everyone else is doing it," stop and think about the absurdity of this statement. When we are doing something because everyone else is doing it, we are likely influenced by the herd instinct.

"I don't give a damn for any man who can spell a word only one way."

- Mark Twain

It is easy to follow the herd. Being different is difficult because people will criticize and dislike you for having the courage to show your uniqueness. However, you will have your self-respect. You will also have the respect of your critics when you stand out, and succeed in areas in which the herd has no chance of succeeding.

You may have noticed that people in the mainstream don't fare very well in the long run. People who make a difference in any industry or field of endeavor are invariably different. Here are four examples of people who have made a big difference by being different:

* Anita Roddick
* Margaret Thatcher
* Nelson Mandela
* Richard Branson

Anita Roddick is a lot different in many ways than most business owners. For example, she gives her employees a paid half-day off each week to volunteer at a charity or other non-profit organization. Roddick is the founder of the Body Shop, the largest and most profitable cosmetics company in Great Britain which also operates in Canada. The company is as well known in Britain, and almost as well known in Canada, as Coca-Cola and McDonald's are in the U.S. Anita Roddick doesn't have an MBA and probably succeeded because she doesn't have one. She says: "We survived because we have no rational business knowledge."

Margaret Thatcher was the longest reigning British Prime Minister this century. It is interesting to note that Margaret Thatcher was chosen second behind Adolf Hitler as the person, past or present, most hated in a 1988 poll conducted by Madame Tussaud's Waxworks Museum in London, England. In 1983, she was chosen fourth, and in 1978, she was chosen third. She was hated, but she was respected. She was liked as well; she had to be to get elected in three consecutive elections.

In 1994, Nelson Mandela became South Africa's first black president after successfully attaining his goal of eliminating apartheid in his country. In the 1960s, he was convicted of sabotage and treason during his fight against apartheid. After spending 27 years in jail, he was freed. Mandela's willingness to pay the price for being different led the way for his remarkable ascent to power.

Richard Branson is dismissed by British businessmen as a "flake." Over the last few years, they have tried to discredit Branson at every turn. Branson's Virgin Atlantic Airways, against which British Airways conducted an unsuccessful smear campaign, captured $750 million in revenue in the British market. His airline stands for youth, independence, and cheekiness; these are also the traits of his favorite character - Peter Pan.

Richard Branson is definitely different, but highly successful and admired by the British public. BBC Radio conducted a poll to find out who should be charged with rewriting the Ten Commandments. Branson came in at fourth place after Mother Teresa, the Pope, and the Archbishop of Canterbury. Without question, all the businessmen who call Branson a flake would give their left arms to have the popularity and respect Branson has with the British public.

> *"We forfeit three-fourths of ourselves to be like other people."*
>
> *- Arthur Schopenhauer*

Note that if you want to attain even a sliver of the public recognition that Branson has attained, you aren't going to attain any fame in life by trying to fit in with the rest of the pack. I personally have received a modest amount of publicity with well over 100 items comprised of newspaper articles, national TV interviews, radio talk shows, and magazine features about my books and lifestyle. This free publicity probably would have cost me in the neighborhood of $200,000 if I had to buy equivalent advertising space for my books. Of course, paid advertising wouldn't have been as credible and effective. The point is this valuable publicity wasn't a result of my trying to fit in with the rest of the pack.

> *"For my thoughts are not your thoughts, neither are your ways my ways."*
>
> *- The Bible (Isaiah 55:8)*

Just getting your 15 minutes of fame, as promised by Andy Warhol, will be extremely difficult if you are a carbon copy of everyone else. The news media isn't in the business of gratuitously writing about just anyone - the news media is in the business of providing interesting stories for its readers. I found out long ago that the chances for the news media writing about me are increased dramatically if I follow these principles:

- Be first
- Be different
- Be daring

> *"All great ideas are controversial, or have been at one time."*
>
> *- George Seldes*

Dick Drew, host of the national network radio program called *The Canadian Achievers* and author of the book with the same name, has the following lengthy quotation printed on his business card. I have found the quotation to be empowering, and carry Drew's business card with me so that I can read the quotation from time to time.

"If you follow the crowd, you will likely get no further than the crowd. If you walk alone, you're likely to end up in places no one has ever been before.

Being an achiever is not without its difficulties, for peculiarity breeds contempt. The unfortunate thing about being ahead of your time is that when people finally realize you were right, they'll simply say it was obvious to everyone all along.

You have two choices in life. You can dissolve into the main stream, or you can choose to become an achiever and be distinct. To be distinct, you must be different. To be different, you must strive to be what no else but you can be."

If you are always trying to fit in because you want to be liked by everyone, you may wind up getting liked just a little bit by most people, but not liked a lot by anyone. You will certainly never attain great recognition or any fame by following the herd. You are unique and deserve unique treatment; so why are you trying to be the same as everyone else?

Be Reasonable And Have An Unreasonable Day

"It will never work because it's a dumb idea! Everyone will think you are weird." If you have had a significantly different idea, chances are that you were told it would never work by colleagues, friends, or family. Society and our educational institutions programmed us to be reasonable. The problem is we become too reasonable. Our voices of judgment promptly label many ideas "unreasonable," when, in fact, the ideas may have great merit. Being unreasonable, and doing what others wouldn't consider, can generate remarkable results as the following two examples indicate:

> *"Where all men think alike, no one thinks very much."*
>
> *- Walter Lippmann*

In 1989, Tennessee resident Jane Berzynsky read a tabloid's account of actor Bob Cummings's fourth divorce. She decided to be unreasonable and write to him, although she had never met him or talked to him on the phone. In her letter, she said that she was available if he wanted to consider a relationship with her. A photo was also included with the letter. Cummings, a Gemini, checked Berzynsky's Aquarius sign out with his astrologer. She checked out astrologically okay so he flew her to Los Angeles. Jane Berzynsky ended up becoming Bob Cummings's fifth wife because she was willing to do something that was considered unreasonable by most people.

Here is the second example: In April, 1995 radio host Pierre Brassard of CKOI-FM in Montreal also did something totally unreasonable. He decided to call the Vatican in an attempt to talk to Pope John Paul. This is unreasonable considering even a high ranking Cardinal in Montreal said he wouldn't ever think of trying to call the Pope. Brassard's staff ended up getting the Pope on the line by using a little deceit (the staff chose to call it creativity). They claimed Brassard was Jean Chretien, the Prime Minister of Canada.

A telephone conversation spoken in French between Brassard and the Pope lasted about 18 minutes; it was mostly small talk going nowhere. At one point Brassard asked the Pope when he was going to get a propeller for his cap, but the Pope didn't seem to understand the question. Reporters from media outlets all around North America were envious of what Brassard had done. Many other radio stations then tried to get an interview with the Pope, but to no avail. Producers from TNN and the David Letterman show ended up calling CKOI-FM wanting to get a tape of the conversation between Brassard and the Pope.

> *"Don't worry about people stealing your ideas. If your ideas are any good, you'll have to ram them down people's throats."*
>
> *- Howard Aiken*

We are all victims of our voices of judgment, the rational part of us that can jump in and destroy an idea before it has a chance to blossom. Many good ideas aren't given any chance. We tend to find something negative about these ideas and promptly discard them. The reverse is also true. We may promptly accept an idea without looking at all the negatives. Our voices of judgment work to classify things as black and white. We end up spending 95 percent of our time judging people and events whether they are bad or good, and right or wrong.

If you designate one day every week as your unreasonable day, and go through that day challenging your voice of judgment, you will notice life is different. I have selected Thursday as my unreasonable day. On Thursdays, I continually question my voice of judgment. With all the success I have had in arranging interviews that I initially thought I couldn't get, and getting to know people I didn't think I could meet, I have concluded it is very reasonable to be unreasonable. Here are some unreasonable things to do on your unreasonable day:

> *"Let's drink a toast to folly and to dreams because they are the only reasonable things."*
>
> *- From The Green King by Paul-Loup Sulitzer*

* Try to obtain phone numbers of three members of the opposite sex you would like to meet
* If you know someone who has the ideal job, and would like to talk to them, telephone them on your unreasonable day
* Surprise someone with a totally different deed or gift

* Say something complimentary to the cashier at the grocery or
  department store
* Learn to go against the trend in whatever you are doing or
  trying to accomplish

The Most Important Creativity Principle

As already indicated, being creative is essential for you to live
happily as a single. Creativity is an important force to help us be
truly alive. The highly creative individual is constantly discovering
new events, finding new ways of doing things, and arriving at new
insights in life. If you are newly single, getting in touch with your
creativity will help you to remodel your identity and rediscover your
essence.

Creative people are flexible people. Taoism extols the virtue of
flexibility. What survives on earth is what effortlessly adapts to the
changing environment and changing circumstances. Your ability to
be flexible will help you change plans in midstream, respond to the
unexpected at a moment's notice, or rearrange a schedule without
experiencing emotional turmoil.

We must remember how crucial
imagination is for success in life. Being
creative goes hand in hand with having a
healthy attitude. In any field of endeavor,
imaginative people are most successful over
the long term. They see opportunity, where
others see insurmountable problems.
Creative individuals take action in a difficult
situation, instead of complaining about it.
Utilizing one's creativity determines a great
range of life's successes including acquiring
promotions, experiencing happiness,
developing meaningful relationships, and
maintaining physical and emotional health.

Your Singles Advantage

* **You can be as messy as your mood allows**
* **You get to decorate your home with wild colors**

So, start being more creative right now.
Look for many solutions. Be unreasonable
one day or more every week. Be silly. Think
way out in left field. You'll be much happier

and better off as a single. The whole world will also be a better place when you choose to be creative.

By the way, there is one more creativity principle in addition to the 17 previously mentioned. The last principle is the most important: Ignore all the principles of creativity that don't apply in your life. Who says that there has to be a right or wrong way to be creative? Other techniques exist. Your objective is to enhance your ability to see and generate more options in your life by using as many techniques as possible.

"Any powerful idea is absolutely fascinating and absolutely useless until we choose to use it."

- From "One" By Richard Bach

Solutions To Exercise

1. Move one of the match sticks from the II to get **III + I = IV** (Note that since either match stick can be moved, this constitutes two solutions).

2. Move one of the match sticks from the III to get **II + II = IV** (This translates into three solutions since either of three match sticks can be moved).

3. Move the vertical match stick from IV to get **III + II = V**.

4. Move one of the match sticks from the V to get **IIII - II = I** (The last match stick remains slanted).

5. Move the match stick from the plus sign to get **IIIIII = IV**. Now look at this in the mirror which reads **VI = IIIIII**. To make both sides equal count the number of match sticks on the right side of the equation which gives **VI = six**.

6. Take the vertical match stick from IV, break it in half, and then use the halves to create **-III - II = -V**.

7. Take one of the match sticks from the V and light it up. Then burn the remaining one from the V and throw the first lit one away to end up with **III-II = I**.

8. Move one of the match sticks from the III and move over the = sign to end up with **II - II ≠ IV**.

6. How To Creatively Loaf Your Life Away

Being A Creative Loafer Isn't Easy

"Hey baby, what's in your soul?
You got the silver, you got the gold.
You got the diamonds from the mine,
Well that's all right, can you buy some time?"

- You Got The Silver © by Mick Jagger/ Keith Richards

A *"Bizarro"* cartoon by Dan Piraro shows a male patient talking to a Doctor in the physician's office. The patient asks the Doctor: "When I touch my tongue to aluminum foil wrapped around a walnut while holding a toaster oven, I feel a peculiar tingling in my toes ..... What's wrong with me Doctor?" The Doctor replies: "You have too much spare time."

Whether, retired, unemployed, or working, many singles have a problem with their spare time. If you haven't developed an ability to be truly leisurely, the day that you retire is the day you will be saying to yourself: "Okay, what does a genius like me do now?" You may end up

> *"I shall marry in haste and repent in leisure."*
>
> *- James Branch Cahell*

feeling that the leisurely lifestyle is the biggest rip-off since the last time you got conned into buying the Golden Gate Bridge or swampland in Florida. As odd as it may seem, being a creative loafer isn't easy; what it takes is some effort or work. This shouldn't be a surprise - The Easy Rule Of Life applies to leisure as well.

95

"Sometimes I get an irresistible urge to work hard like you two guys, but I just lie down until the feeling goes away, and then I am okay again."

If you have read *"The Joy Of Not Working,"* and feel that you have mastered the art of handling your leisure time, you can skip this chapter. Note, although this chapter covers a few of the same topics as my book on how to enjoy leisure time like never before, it throws some new light on these topics with different content, quotations, and cartoons.

Handling leisure time effectively is important for singles. In relationships, leisure activities such as tennis, reading, and jogging are usually the first to go. Generally speaking, singles should have more opportunity than attached individuals to pursue their leisure interests. One danger of being single is having the tendency to substitute a job for a relationship; many singles get married to their jobs and wind up becoming workaholics. Trying to get to the top of the heap requires extra time that could be leisurely spent cultivating intimate relationships or canoeing down some lazy river.

How To Be A Connoisseur Of Leisure

Elizabeth Custer, Private Time Editor for *Glamour* magazine, recently telephoned me from New York to solicit my opinion on why the magazine's readers indicated in a survey that they are usually more exhausted on Sundays than they are on Fridays. Surprised by the survey's results, I had to give some thought to the question before I could give an adequate answer.

"All work and no play makes Jack a dull boy - and Jill a wealthy widow."

- Evan Esar

The answer lies in the Protestant work ethic. Someone visiting from another planet would think that most human beings must have serious kinks in their brains to utilize their leisure the way they do. Due to the Protestant work ethic, many people feel anxiety or guilt when they try to relax. Instead, they get busy doing things. Weekends are used to attend to miscellaneous chores and personal business. Time is spent on repairing houses, mowing lawns, and caring for children. Weekend busyness adds to the burnout already experienced during the work week. Due to the self-imposed demands on their time, people are spending less time on the basics, such as sleeping and eating. It is no wonder that workers feel more exhausted on Sunday then they do on Friday.

Your Singles Advantage

- **All messages on the telephone answering machine are yours**
- **It is easier to be spontaneous**

Leisure is supposed to take care of itself on weekends and when we retire. Nothing is further from the truth. We are socialized to work hard and to feel guilty about not working. Many people are afraid of free time, or just plainly don't know how to enjoy it. Some researchers say most Americans don't want more leisure time; they only get meaning and satisfaction from doing things.

Discipline and a certain attitude are required to utilize leisure time wisely. To be a connoisseur of leisure, you must regularly stop and smell the roses. Leisure should transcend just being a time to rest for the sake of one's work. True leisure time is spent at activities such as intimate conversation, tennis, sex, or watching a sunset; it is for the sake of enjoying the activity itself. True leisure is anything which is done for sheer pleasure, and not so one can be more productive at work.

If you can't think of any leisure activities to enjoy, you are working too hard, and haven't spent enough time getting to know yourself. It is never too late for you to develop a new interest, or learn a new sport or skill. Start by writing down the things that you would like to pursue in your life before you die. Your list may be based on things you like doing now, things you loved doing in the past but have quit doing, and things you thought about doing but have never tried. Think of all the things in life which you love; then, in some way relate

"There are three things difficult: to suffer an injury; to keep a secret; and to use leisure."

- Voltaire

them to leisure activities which you can pursue. Here is a list created by the British writer Agatha Christie (1890-1976) as included in the book *"Agatha Christie: An Autobiography"* (Dodd, Mead & Co., 1977). This list may trigger some of the things that turn you on.

- ♥ Sunshine
- ♥ Apples
- ♥ Almost any kind of music
- ♥ Railway trains
- ♥ Numerical puzzles and anything to do with numbers
- ♥ Going to the sea
- ♥ Bathing and swimming
- ♥ Silence
- ♥ Sleeping
- ♥ Dreaming
- ♥ Eating
- ♥ The smell of coffee
- ♥ Lilies of the valley
- ♥ Most dogs
- ♥ Going to the theatre

"Few women and fewer men have enough character to be idle."

- E.V. Lucas

Note that quality leisure is dependent upon being engaged in at least a few active activities which involve risk and challenge. Passive activities, such as watching television and shopping, won't provide much satisfaction. Examples of active activities are reading, writing, exercising, taking a course, and learning a new language. Because these activities involve some risk and challenge, they are more enjoyable and satisfying.

If you are in the work force, having the ability to enjoy not working may come in handy at various times during your working years. Here are four reasons why you should have the ability to enjoy leisure to the fullest:

Four Reasons To Be A Connoisseur Of Leisure

- If you go to a job interview desperate for the job, your desperation is likely to be noticed by job interviewers. Being happy without a job puts you in a much better frame of mind while you are job hunting. If you aren't desperate for a job, your positive attitude will show, and you will stand a much greater chance of being hired for the job.

- With high rates of unemployment here to stay, most people will experience more, and longer periods, of unemployment. Hence, it only makes sense to learn to be as happy as we possibly can without a job.
- If you base your identity on your work, you lose yourself when you lose your job. When your identity is based on other elements, you have your identity with or without a job.
- If you learn how to be happy without a job, you won't be as afraid of losing your job when you get another one. You will be confident that you can still find life enjoyable regardless of your situation.

Many futurists are now predicting that work as we have known it since the industrial revolution is likely to be virtually phased out. As more robots and computers are used to replace human labor, less work will be available for the general population. The future will demand that you learn how to be a connoisseur of leisure.

> *"Give a man a fish and he eats for a day. Teach him how to fish and you get rid of him for the whole weekend."*
>
> *- Zenna Schaffer*

Are the TV, Couch, and Fridge Your Three Best Friends?

Surveys indicate that North Americans utilize an incredible 40 percent of their leisure time watching television - no wonder people have insufficient time for exercising, visiting friends, and watching sunsets. The North American adult between 18 and 65 has 40 hours of spare time a week, and spends 16 hours of it in front of the tube. In comparison, only two hours are spent reading and four hours are spent talking to relatives, friends, and acquaintances.

Ironically, on a list of 22 leisure activities, TV viewing rated seventeenth on the amount of enjoyment and satisfaction attained. Reading was rated ninth on this list. Why do people watch television if they get so little satisfaction from the activity? People choose television viewing because it is the easy thing to do. Of course, due to television's low rate of return in terms of satisfaction, the easy route turns out to be difficult and uncomfortable in the long term.

> *"If a man watches three football games in a row, he should be declared legally dead."*
>
> *- Erma Bombeck*

TV-free America is a newly established national organization based in Washington which raises awareness of the harmful effects of excessive television watching. The organization recommends that, instead of watching television, people should spend their time in more productive activities, such as contemplating life, playing sports, attending community events, and volunteering. If you are addicted to television, it is time to join a support group such as Couch Potatoes (see resources). Getting away from the television set and into activities promoted by the Institute of Totally Useless Skills - feather balancing, paper-airplane making, napkin stunts, pen bouncing, creative beer-can crushing, or generating symptoms of false physical self-abuse - will do you more good than watching most television programs.

Because you are a single who wants to get the most out of life, one of the most important activities on your leisure list should be exercising to maintain a high level of fitness and wellness. Developing a positive relationship with your body will pay off handsomely. How you look physically is important to how you feel about yourself, and how others feel about you. Having a fit and trim body will raise your self-respect and command the respect of others.

The University of California *Wellness Letter* stated in 1992 that 18 percent of people in Montana and 52 percent of people in the District of Columbia had reported no participation in any leisure-time physical activity during the previous month. I become disgusted with myself if I have no leisure-time physical activity for two days, let alone a month. A few years ago, I thought I could get away with eating like a horse and not exercising. Darn it - no such luck! I found out, when the post office was about to give me my own postal code because of my size, that eating excessively, and not exercising, was going to cost me a new wardrobe, not to mention the not-so-insignificant items of health and wellness. For the last 15 years, I have exercised twice a day, for a total of at least two hours, by participating in vigorous activities such as tennis, jogging, and cycling. Of course, some lazy, unfit people now tell me how lucky I am because I don't have a weight problem.

If the television, the couch, and the fridge have become your three best friends, you must take action now. Establish a fitness program and stick to it. You will be developing the qualities of commitment, perseverance, and patience by adhering to your program. These same qualities will assist you in achieving satisfaction in other aspects of your single life. Maintaining a healthy lifestyle makes the other important things in life attainable. Treat your body with respect. Don't overeat, and try to exercise on a regular basis. By regular, I don't mean once every two weeks or once a week. Exercise rigorously every day - no exceptions - and you will see a nice return on your investment. Dr. Wayne Dyer, in his fifties, runs ten miles a day and has done this for something like 15 years without missing even one day. That shows commitment.

Your Singles Advantage

- **Can hang your canoe in your living room without having a spouse complain**
- **No need to see a marriage counselor**

Forget about all the shortcuts to being fit and trim. Conditioning requires time and effort. If you keep saying: "As soon as I get some free time, I'll start exercising," you aren't likely to ever get around to exercising. Saying that you have no time for fitness is saying you have no time for health. You have to create time and be committed to being fit. How are you going to get the time? Easy! If you watch television two hours a day, just quit watching television. Now you have two hours for exercise.

You must learn to get fit on your own, and not use the excuse that you don't have anyone to exercise with. If you work at a regular job, another excuse that may pop up is that after work you are too tired to exercise. The problem with this excuse is that often you need exercise the most when you don't feel like exercising. Normally, you are feeling mental fatigue; this will be alleviated by physical exercise. Half the battle is just getting out there for the first ten minutes. After that, the next 45 minutes or an hour are relatively easy. Other excuses that people use are: exercising is boring, I am too old to begin, it's too cold outside, I am twenty years old and don't need to

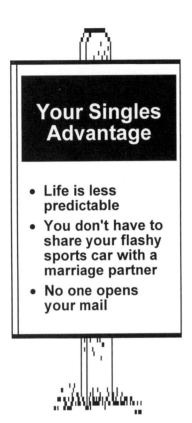

Your Singles Advantage

- **Life is less predictable**
- **You don't have to share your flashy sports car with a marriage partner**
- **No one opens your mail**

exercise, and I don't want to sustain an injury. If you use any of these excuses, you are just fooling yourself. These are excuses and not reasons. You are using the excuses to cover up your laziness.

Establish a regular routine for exercising. If you have a hard time being alone, join a fitness club and you will be killing two birds - getting fit and socializing - with one stone. Get involved in more than one activity which will get you fit. This provides variety and alternatives if you can't do one of the activities on a particular day. And don't forget to reward yourself when you have attained your fitness goals.

The time to start exercising is now. Being fit gives you the following benefits: reduces stress, helps you sleep better, helps to reduce weight, increases self-esteem, slows down aging, improves sexual performance, reduces chances of heart disease, and improves agility. Of course, you will be much more attractive to members of the opposite sex.

A Saner Lifestyle In Which Less Is More

The people of Greece, who are not as rich as those in most of the other countries comprising the European Common Market, have a saying: "When you are poor, it is important to have a good time." The point is a good time isn't dependent on having a large sum of money. This was recently confirmed by researchers at the University of Chicago who conducted a study on which activities people most enjoyed. The researchers found that people received the most satisfaction out of activities which cost the least money. Activities which cost nothing or very little, such as going for a walk in the woods, were more satisfying than costly activities, such as going to movies or expensive restaurants.

Opting out of the rat race, and putting more leisure time into your days, can lead to a far richer life. Less can be more. It takes courage and trust in one's intuition to make a dramatic change in one's life, and to forego security and a great deal of money in the process.

My friend Jim Mackenzie is a school teacher who gets more out of life by taking a sabbatical about every five years. At the time of my writing this book, Jim is taking a year off with no particular plan in mind. His destination is unknown, although he would like to go to Africa for a month or two. Jim has found that less is more; less work means more time for living.

A sabbatical is a great way to enjoy life to the fullest. Seriously consider taking a sabbatical, so you can surround yourself with different people, and look at the world with a new pair of eyes. If you haven't taken more than a three-week vacation for years, now is the time to experience a different world. If you have always wanted to move to Paris to become part of the sidewalk-cafe crowd, then take that sabbatical and do it.

The sabbatical isn't only for the rich. Although I haven't made a great deal of money over the years, I have had to work only half of my adult life. The other half has been spent going to university, or taking sabbaticals of various kinds. Be creative in designing a lifestyle with few material wants, and you will increase your ability to monetarily afford to take a sabbatical.

Here is part of a letter (the remaining portion is in Chapter 9) that I received in 1991 from Rita in Vancouver who decided to take a sabbatical from work by quitting her job.

Dear Mr. Zelinski;

I have just finished reading your book The Joy Of Not Working (yes, I did all the exercises too). I love it! Congratulations on a fantastic book.

I had been teaching 7 days a week, 6-12 hours a day without a holiday at a music school for the last 12 years. I originally took the job to earn my way through my Commerce degree, but I continued to habitually work after my graduation 5 years ago.

The job was ruining my life - so I "retired" (after all, I'm still in my twenties) two months ago. Although I was happy with my decision, I was not prepared for my new lifestyle. My friends and colleagues severely criticized me, and I had to find new ways to spend my extra time.

Having read your book, I am convinced that I made the right decision. I am now even proud to be not working.

Yours truly,

Rita

I had the opportunity to talk to Rita about six months after she wrote to me. Her sabbatical from the workplace had done her a lot of good. She said that she was back at work, but working fewer hours, enjoying herself more, and being more productive.

Is Time On Your Side?

In the book *"The Little Prince"* by Antoine de Saint Exupery, the little prince arrives from a foreign planet to visit the planet earth. One of the strange people the little prince encounters is a merchant who tries to sell him pills which allow people to quench their thirst and feel no need to drink anything for a week. The little prince asks the merchant why he is selling these pills. The merchant replies: "Because they save a tremendous amount of time. Computations have been made by experts. With these pills, you save fifty-three minutes in every week."

"Yesterday is a cancelled check; tomorrow is a promissory note; today is the only cash you have - so spend it wisely."

- Kay Lyons

The little prince then asks: "And what do I do with those fifty-three minutes?" and the merchant replies: "Anything you like ....." The little prince in bewilderment says to himself: "As for me, if I had fifty-three minutes to spend as I liked, I should walk at my leisure toward a spring of fresh water."

This story has a lot to say about how we use our time and approach life. In North America, there never seems to be enough time. In this do-it-all society, people drive fast, walk fast, dine fast, and talk fast. Time is so precious that people don't even have a moment to think about time. Even leisure time is experienced in a hurried state. No one can ride a horse, smoke a cigarette, read a book, and make love all at the same time. Yet, it seems many singles are trying to do just that. People have become so involved in controlling time that they can't find the time to enjoy the present moment. Because they don't have a moment to spare, they are less spontaneous, and unable to enjoy the here and now.

Busyness doesn't mean you are in control. Being in the now means opening yourself to the moment in which there are no other moments. Thinking how much happier you would be if only you were in a relationship isn't the way to enjoy life in the here and now. Waiting for something to happen so you can enjoy life means you aren't fully conscious of the world around you. Waiting for a relationship to appear, so you can enjoy life, will result in your postponing the joys of living. If you can immerse yourself in the things you enjoy now, you will be happier now. You will start living in the moment, instead of just existing in a semi-conscious state.

"Just watching people work makes me tired. Because the two of you have been working so hard, I am terribly exhausted and have to immediately leave for home to take my afternoon nap."

Get involved in the process, instead of the end result, and you will know that you are fully experiencing the moment. Learn to let go of the clock. Quiet and uninterrupted time is necessary to reduce the pressure and stresses of modern day life. When you are relaxed, you will be more positive in your outlook on life. Being unhurried means being different from the crowd. You are able to enjoy the magic of the now.

A good way to miss the moment is to spend your time worrying about yesterday and tomorrow. There are many things to worry about. People have nervous breakdowns due to seemingly insignificant things, such as the television breaking down before the start of Oprah, or having lost a few bucks in an investment scam. Some people even worry if they have nothing to worry about.

The key is to put problems and worrying into proper perspective. Always thinking about the future, and postponing things instead of doing them today, means you are missing out on living today. If you think you will be happy in the future when you get to do something

Your Singles Advantage

- If you win a trip for two to Hawaii, you can go twice
- Studies show single people sleep better than married people

drastically different, you're fooling yourself. Now is the time to be happy. Worrying about retirement, and putting things off until then, is risky since you don't know if you will reach retirement age. Save your energy for the truly serious problems you have to solve. Fill your life with hope, dreams, and creative leisure instead of worry.

Leisureholics Have More Fun

You can bring your life under control, and put it in better balance, by reorienting yourself to a new relationship with leisure. By deciding to be a leisureholic, instead of a workaholic, you will have more fun in life. Remember that you may be undermining your chances for a meaningful relationship if you are spending too much time at work, and little time in leisure activities. Community life and the quality of your work will also suffer. Also keep in mind that you don't know anyone who on his or her death bed said: "I wish I would have worked more."

Being fully alive means being able to experience the moment. Life will take on a more exciting quality when you learn how to be more leisurely and conscious of the moment. Being in the here and now is learning to pay attention to the world around you in order that you have control over the important events in your life. Experiencing the now in your leisure activities will mean each day will be enhanced with richness and intrigue.

"I would not exchange my leisure hours for all the wealth in the world."

- Comte de Mirabeau

Leisure activities provide unlimited opportunities for growth and satisfaction. As a single, you should have more freedom to create the time to pursue constructive leisure activities. The big advantage of being single is you get to design your work schedule, your leisure time, your friendships, and your relationships for a lifestyle which is truly your own.

7. Leave Me Alone Or I Will Find Someone Who Will

"You Grow Only When You Are Alone"

"When from our better selves we have too long
Been parted by the hurrying world, and droop,
Sick of its business, of its pleasures tired,
How gracious, how benign, is Solitude."

- From The Prelude by William Wordsworth

To truly experience the joy of not being married, you must learn how to appreciate your time alone. Time alone is an opportunity to learn and grow as a person. Being alone is also the time to unplug from the hectic pace of life with others. The Hindus have a powerful Proverb: "You grow only when you are alone." As a single individual, you need time alone as an opportunity to get to know yourself better. Solitude is for thinking through those philosophical issues that affect your life.

The lone cowboy or explorer can capture our fascination. These people are alone for a purpose. They may be alone, but not lonely. If you have read *"Illusions,"* Richard Bach flying solo in his barnstorming airplane may have led you to romanticize this independent person who has the freedom to wander at will.

> *"If you are afraid of loneliness, do not marry."*
>
> *- Chekhov*

"Would you like to come over to my apartment and see my wine cork and bread tab collections?"

"Ted, I think that you have been living alone for too long."

Solitude can be a great inspiration to the creative artist. It is an opportunity for renewal and reflection. The majority of painters, sculptors, poets, writers, and composers spend most of their time alone because they can be much more creative and get more done.

Some singles seek being alone; other singles have solitude thrust upon them. For well-balanced singles, solitude is essential to maintain a strong sense of self. Their motto is: "Leave me alone or I will find someone who will." Solitude often is preferred over having company. Many well-balanced singles appreciate being alone while painting a picture or going for a walk. Their friends are often surprised that at times they prefer solace over companionship. People who at times choose being alone over companionship aren't loners; they are usually happy in the company of others, but they regularly need some time alone.

Well-balanced individuals, whether single or attached, cherish their time alone because solitude is an opportune time for personal growth. Many people in solid relationships will extol the importance of solitude for a strong sense of self. I know several individuals in healthy marriages who treasure their solitude. These attached people spend time alone in separate rooms, in leisure activities, or even on long vacations taken separately, without hindering the relationship. In fact, relationships seem to be enhanced by the time that well-balanced partners spend apart. Perhaps, more relationships would be more successful if the partners spent more time alone.

"One of the greatest necessities in America is to discover creative solitude."

- Carl Sandburg

The flip side of satisfying solitude is loneliness. Many singles can't handle being alone for even the shortest period of time. They flip on the television, or tune into a radio talk show, the moment they enter their homes. Elvis Presley, like many lonely people, hated being alone and turned on a television in any deserted room he entered. The problem with watching a great deal of television alone is television may become a poor substitute for a sense of community. When this happens, relationships with friends, relatives, and acquaintances suffer.

Other unhealthy ways to handle loneliness are sleeping, getting stoned, boozing, gambling, and shopping. In the short term, these responses seem to help alleviate loneliness. However, these responses don't alleviate loneliness in the long run, because they don't enhance social skills, help form close relationships, or develop high self-esteem.

> *"I find it wholesome to be alone the greater part of the time. To be in company, even with the best, is soon wearisome and dissipating. I love to be alone. I never found the companion that was so companionable as solitude."*
>
> - *Thoreau*

A recent study by *Psychology Today* magazine indicated that over 50 percent of people in the United States suffer from loneliness, either sometimes or often. This means that loneliness is common with over 100 million people in the U.S. This may come as a shock to many singles, but married people suffer from loneliness as much, if not more, than single people. Lonely married people may actually suffer more, because the excuse that they don't have a marriage partner no longer applies. It is important to accept that finding a marriage partner won't cure anyone of loneliness. Loneliness is not caused by being single, divorced, or separated.

Chronic loneliness is suffered by people with low self-esteem. Individuals having certain traits - lack of identity, perfectionism, fear of rejection, inability to take risks, feelings of inadequacy, and lack of social skills - are most prone to chronic loneliness. The irony is that people who aren't comfortable with themselves normally make poor friends or lovers because they have self-esteem problems. They are needy and cling desperately to others. Clingers hungry for love and acceptance have a hard time with rejection. Ironically, they end up being rejected with greater frequency, because most individuals are turned off by needy people.

People not in touch with themselves are very uncomfortable being alone for any length of time. Note that even the most successful singles will have at least some loneliness to contend with. What all singles require are strategies for spending time alone.

"If You Are Lonely When You Are Alone, You Are In Bad Company"

"We're all in this alone."

- Lily Tomlin

Whether you choose to be happy or sad while you are alone will depend on your attitude. The rewards of solitude can't be experienced by people with a negative attitude about being alone. Changing your attitude about being alone will mean that you look forward to solitude. If you feel lonely when you are alone, you are out of touch with the world around you. You are also out of touch with yourself. Keep in mind the words of Jean-Paul Sartre: "If you are lonely when you're alone, you are in bad company." All well-balanced individuals - single or married - cherish their time alone because they are in great company when they are with themselves.

Having to spend a lot of time alone doesn't make you an inferior person. If you have difficulty being alone, you will have to put more effort into enjoying the time you spend by yourself. It takes effort and practice to make a relationship work, and it takes effort and practice to make being alone work. Don't fall into the trap of thinking that you are incapable of dealing with loneliness. Thinking thoughts like, "I am alone and lonely because I'll never fit in," will be self-defeating and just support you in remaining alone and lonely. You are helpless because you choose to be helpless.

If you spend little time at home, and treat your apartment like a hotel room - a place only to change clothes and sleep - then you have to learn how to enjoy yourself more. You can't go on saying: "If only I were attached, I wouldn't get lonely." Paradoxically, you will be undermining your chances for a meaningful relationship if you don't learn how to be happy alone. The key to attracting a well-balanced partner is to learn to live with, and for, yourself first. You have to be comfortable with who you are as an individual. Not learning how to handle being alone can lead you - out of desperation - to spend time with inappropriate members of the opposite sex. The danger is that you will wind up in a relationship which is just a less-than-satisfying

"The great misfortune - to be incapable of solitude."

- Jean de la Bruyere

110

compromise to help you fill the empty spaces.

Although your ideal situation is to be in a loving, intimate relationship, you are better off being alone, and happy to a substantial degree, instead of being involved in a relationship which is nothing more than a dull compromise. Why get trapped in a relationship which is likely to bring you a great deal of unhappiness? Learning to be happy alone will give you the confidence and patience to wait for someone more appropriate to come along and be your dating or marriage partner.

The single lifestyle, as compared to the married lifestyle, offers the luxury of more time to spend in solitude. This may not necessarily be true for singles with young children, but, generally speaking, this holds for most singles. Singles don't have as much of an obligation to socialize, if they don't want to. To well-balanced singles, the lack of a marriage partner doesn't dictate that can't enjoy life. Happy singles can do things alone because they know how to practice dynamic solitude.

> *"In losing a husband, one loses a master who is often an obstacle to the enjoyment of many things."*
>
> *- Madeleine de Scudery, French Novelist*

There are many enjoyable ways to spend time alone: painting a picture, going to a movie, writing a book, climbing a mountain, meditating, gardening, traveling to Europe, watching a sunset while sitting on the lake shore, and going for a long walk.

Constructive action is required to deal with loneliness; the solution is to learn how to appreciate solitude. People who learn to appreciate solitude experience their deeper selves. This enhances their relationships with others. In social settings, they are more relaxed and genuine, and have no need to act different from their authentic selves. Singles, who thrive on solitude, tend to develop deeper and more sincere relationships with friends than do singles who are afraid to be alone.

An alternative to being alone is to channel your energy into social action. Go out and spend more time with people. This can entail sharing an activity with people who have formed a close relationship with you. Spending time to create new friendships, volunteering to help others, and reconnecting with old friends and acquaintances are other ways of minimizing your time alone.

Being Happy Alone Today Leads To A Happier Tomorrow

Living single and learning how to be happy alone can be advantageous for handling loneliness in later years. In a February, 1995 article issued by Canadian Press, Judy Creighton reported that Vancouver social workers Gloria Levi and Beryl Petty found that never-married individuals handle old age much better than individuals who are on their own after having lost their spouse through death or divorce. Levi and Petty have studied loneliness associated with growing older in focus groups they lead. They found seniors who have been single all their lives, or for a fairly long time, fare much better in old age. Because they have lived alone a long time, these singles have found ways to attain satisfaction in their lives without a marriage partner.

"The dread of loneliness is greater than the fear of bondage, so we get married."

- From the Unquiet Grave, 1944, by Cyril Connolly

Often older people, especially men, tend to die within a year or two after losing a spouse, unless they find someone else to marry. Older men tend to be ex-workaholics who relied on their wives for support. With the job long gone, and now the wife, these men have a difficult time coping with life in general. Many older women also have a hard time coping as widows, because they relied on their husbands for managing finances, looking after the house maintenance, and making key decisions.

On the other hand, Levi and Petty found that many married men and women, who lose a spouse and learn how to cope being alone, actually are very excited about being alone, once they get over the sadness and grief. These individuals discover their creativity, which they channel into activities such as writing and painting. These new singles also experience freedom and independence which they didn't have in their marriages. This translates into an opportunity to enjoy life like never before.

For Happiness And Longevity, Try Eccentricity

Alan Fairweather of Scotland eats only potatoes, either baked, boiled, or fried. On the rare occasion, he may break this rule and eat a chocolate bar to add variety to his life. Fairweather not only chooses potatoes as the mainstay in his diet - he makes potatoes his life. He works as a potato inspector for the Agricultural Ministry in Scotland. Needless to say, Fairweather loves potatoes.

You are probably thinking: "Fairweather is an eccentric." You are absolutely right. Whatever else you are thinking, don't feel sorry for Fairweather and others like him. Fairweather is a "true" eccentric according to psychologist Dr. David Weeks and writer Jamie James, who both wrote the book *"Eccentrics"* to be published in 1995.

Eccentrics, like potato lover Fairweather, spend a great deal of time alone; however, Weeks and James found that eccentrics are certainly not unhappy people. Quite surprisingly, Weeks and James found that eccentrics are much happier than the rest of the population. They are also healthier and tend to live much longer. And for those of you who think people like Fairweather are crazy, Weeks and James concluded that eccentrics are much more intelligent than the general population. True eccentrics are non-conforming, highly creative, curious, idealistic, intelligent, opinionated, and obsessed with some hobby. Weeks and James studied over 900 eccentrics and found that the majority of these men and women live alone because others find them too peculiar to live with. Nonetheless, spending time alone is not a problem for true eccentrics; they thrive on it.

I initially couldn't think of any true eccentrics I know personally. Later, I thought of someone in Toronto who is considered an eccentric by many Torontonians. He is Ben Kerr, the busker, who was first mentioned in Chapter 4. Ben is well-known in the city because he runs for mayor of Toronto whenever the mayoralty race occurs every four years or so. Besides not being employed in the traditional sense, Ben isn't married, although he once was.

> *"My personal hobbies are reading, listening to music, and silence."*
>
> *- Dame Edith Sitwell*

In 1982, Ben Kerr was married and successful according to society's definition of success. He quit his job as an assistant credit manager with the Toronto Harbour Commission after an office reorganization left him sitting beside a man who smoked cigarettes. Because Kerr couldn't stand the smoke, he quit when no one in higher management responded to his concerns. He took his campaign against smoking to Nashville and Los Angeles. Upon returning to Toronto in 1983, he decided to end his unfulfilled marriage. Ever since then, he has remained single and hasn't worked for anyone else. Shortly after I told Ben that I was writing this book, he came up with his song called *"The Joy Of Not Being Married."* These are the words to the song:

"Once in a while you have to take a break and visit yourself."

- Audrey Giorgi

The Joy Of Not Being Married

The joy of not being married
The joy of being truly free
The joy of not being married
Is the next thing to heaven for me.

I can stay out all night long if I want to
And not have to use the telephone
To lie to a wife with a story
Why tonight I won't be coming home

The joy of not being married
To do as I please every day
The joy of not being married
Living the bachelor way

I can write a love song when I want to
'Bout a woman who comes into my life
And not have to face the fury
Of a jealous, unforgiving wife

The joy of not being married
The joy of being truly free
The joy of not being married
Is the next thing to heaven for me

The joy of not being married
Is the next thing to heaven for me

© 1995 by Ben Kerr

114

If you are ever in Toronto, head down to Yonge and Bloor between two and five o'clock in the afternoon, and ask Ben to sing this song or *"The Joy Of Not Working Nine To Five"* to you. Tell him I sent you. You will meet a most interesting and happy individual.

Eccentrics like Ben Kerr have a lot of freedom, a luxury which many singles have. They are free to pursue hobbies and lifestyles which are their passions. Freed from the need to conform, eccentrics aren't bothered by what others think of them. Their important traits, especially self-confidence and a sense of freedom, help them achieve great happiness and longevity. So, the moral of the story is for happiness and longevity, try eccentricity.

Give Solitude A Chance

Many singles, when confronted with being alone, don't get used to being alone because they don't give solitude a chance. They immediately turn on the television, or spontaneously decide to go shopping for something that they don't need or can't afford. Because they don't give solitude a chance, they never get to appreciate it.

After having been with people for any length of time, we get addicted to having someone around us, especially when we are with quality people. Richard Bach, in his book *"Illusions,"* related how it always took some effort and adjustment to return to being by himself after having been around people for some time. He wrote: "Lonely again. A person gets used to being alone, but break it just for a day and you have to get used to it again."

While writing this book, as well as my previous ones, I had to get used to being alone. For the first fifteen minutes or half-hour, I tended to make phone calls, turn on the radio to a talk show, or read material which had absolutely no use for my projects. I had to first confront the reality that I was alone. Then, I settled into writing, and actually enjoyed being alone.

> *"Get away from the crowd when you can. Keep yourself to yourself, if only for a few hours daily."*
>
> *- Arthur Brisbane*

When you find yourself alone, don't try to escape being alone at the first sign of anxiety or fear. You don't have to feel abandoned or disconnected. Rather than thinking of yourself as being without someone, realize that you are in the company of someone really important - yourself. This is a precious opportunity to pursue the

Your Singles Advantage

- **You can hide your dirty dishes in the closet**
- **You can stay up as long as you want**

rewards that only dynamic solitude has to offer.

We all experience at least a touch of loneliness at some stage in our lives. Even the most successful individuals, whether single or attached, will experience short periods of loneliness. Individuals who are often alone, but don't experience much loneliness, feel good about themselves and their lives. They enjoy their own company as much as that of anyone else. They also know that satisfaction and happiness in life are possible without an intimate relationship.

When I am alone with all my conveniences, such as the telephone, radio, books, computer, magazines, and various forms of transportation, I may feel just a little lonely for a short period of time. But, I remember that highly motivated individuals have experienced long periods of solitary confinement without feeling their lives were meaningless. The true story about Sidney Rittenberg is enough to put my being alone in proper perspective.

Sidney Rittenberg spent 11 years in a Chinese jail, all in solitary confinement. For years, the guards wouldn't even allow Rittenberg to talk to himself; he also wasn't allowed to have a pen and paper to write letters. He said that he kept reminding himself he could be in downtown New York among 10,000 people, and be lonelier than he was in jail all those years. If Sidney Rittenberg can spend 11 years in solitary confinement without any conveniences, and come out of it well-balanced, certainly all of us single people can deal with being alone a few hours a day.

"Knowing others is wisdom, knowing yourself is Enlightenment."

- Lao-tzu

Sidney Rittenberg made the choice not to be lonely in his own company; you can do the same. Possibly the art of loving being alone is the key to being a happy single, as well as meeting someone special down the road. Learning to be happy when you are alone indicates an inner quality and a strong sense of self.

8. Put Money In Its Place

The Chase After Money Is A Chase After Something Else

Two types of singles are continually obsessed with money - those who have a lot of it, and those who don't have a lot of it. When money is involved, common sense seems to go flying out the window. Psychologists have found that many people have more hang-ups about money than they do about sex. Considering all the financial problems human beings have, it would be better if we didn't have to play the money game.

Unfortunately, regardless of how much money we have, we all have to play the money game to some extent. Food, housing, education, transportation, health care, and clothing are all based on having adequate money. Most of us have to expend time, energy, and effort to make a living. This interferes with our enjoyment of the really interesting things that life has to offer.

In North America, money shouldn't be the big problem most people make it out to be. The money game is actually quite easy to play, if you know the secret that was passed on to me sometime ago. The secret is that there are two powerful ways of handling money. If you don't know the secret, I will share the two powerful ways of handling money with you later in this chapter.

> *"Don't marry for money. You can borrow it cheaper."*
>
> *- Unknown Wise Person*

Singles who are satisfying their basic needs in life can alleviate their financial problems by putting the concept of money in its place. Our socioeconomic problems have more to do with values and expectations than with problems with the economy. Most of us can already meet our genuine material needs. We don't have the time to enjoy what we have, and we want more. In all probability, we couldn't find the time to enjoy more things, if we presently don't have time to enjoy what we already have.

> *"I never hated a man enough to give him his diamonds back."*
>
> *- Zsa Zsa Gabor*

The chase for money and material goods is a misdirected effort to make up for what is missing in our lives. This chase undermines some of the things that we already have, such as our relationships. The problem is we judge ourselves by what we can show for our money. By working harder to accumulate more consumer goods, we end up with less time to spend with friends, family, and community. The chase for money and material goods is normally a chase for something else.

When Enough Is Never Enough

A few years ago, the *Wall Street Journal* commissioned the Roper Organization to see how U.S. citizens defined the American Dream, and whether the Dream was attainable. At one time, the American Dream represented liberty. Now, to most people, the American Dream signifies prosperity or being well-off. People feel free insofar as they have access to money.

Reasonable people would guess that a much higher percentage of affluent people said that they were living the American Dream than those who weren't well-off. This wasn't so. Only six percent of those earning $50,000 or more a year said they had attained the Dream as compared to five percent of people earning $15,000 a year or less. Those with incomes of $15,000 a year or less felt that the American Dream could be attained with a median income of $50,000 a year, while those with incomes of $50,000 or more felt that it would take at least $100,000 a year to live the Dream.

Economic growth won't bring more happiness to most middle-class North Americans. What are classified as economic problems are really psychological problems in disguise. The well-being of North Americans is suffering both emotionally and physically, because of the lack of rich human relations, and the lack of time to enjoy what they

> *"The rich man and his daughter are soon parted."*
>
> *- Kin Hubbard*

already have. Well-off individuals often drive themselves to extreme sickness - even death - in the quest for more money. Many people feel empty and deprived after they have achieved great financial success.

In Canada and the U.S., the poverty line is now drawn at a level where the possessions owned by a poor family are considered that of the middle-class or upper-class in many third-world countries. At one time, owning just a black and white TV set was a luxury for the North American middle class. Then, it was a color set. Now, a color set is considered a necessity of life; practically all families below the poverty line own one. Today, if you own two color sets, you probably aren't considered well-off, considering that almost 50 percent of North American households own two or more color television sets.

"When I phoned to let her know I was going to pick her up in my Mercedes, and later showed up in this old Mercedes van, she found out that I wasn't rich and I found out that she didn't have a sense of humor."

In 1957, Americans reported the highest level of satisfaction with their lives that they have ever reported. The level of satisfaction in the 1980s and 1990s was significantly lower, despite the fact that the number of American households which own dishwashers has gone up seven fold, and the percentage of households which own two or more cars has tripled. In the 1990s, the average North American owns and consumes twice as much as the average North American did in the 1950s. Nevertheless, the average North American probably complains twice as much in the 1990s as the average North American did in the 1950s.

The problem is one of greed; most people want to have it all: make a lot of money, have a big house, own two or three cars, and take increasingly exotic vacations in the Caribbean and the Orient. This have-it-all mentality has led to a lower degree of satisfaction, even though people today have more than people of any other generation ever had.

We have been programmed that the best material comforts and long-term security are necessary for happiness. In North America,

> *"My riches consist not in the extent of my possessions but in the fewness of my wants."*
>
> *- J. Brotherton*

like most affluent Western societies, the majority of us are protected from extreme poverty, hunger, disease, and natural catastrophes to a degree that people in previous generations couldn't have imagined. Nevertheless, we complain about how horrible things are if the economy goes into a slight down turn, and a few of us are temporarily unemployed.

Consumption isn't something that comes naturally to human beings. The drive for constantly increasing ownership of material goods is a programmed behavior which showed up with capitalism, the industrial revolution, and the work ethic. Television also plays a role here. Many of the messages television advertising bombards us with can be detrimental to our well-being. We are led to believe that we will be losers or failures if we don't acquire the latest gadgets and trinkets. We are bombarded with images of what sort of people we should be, how we should dress, which gadgets we should own, the type of car we should drive, and the size of house we should live in. Products advertised in commercials promise everything including self-esteem, happiness, and power. Some of us are influenced by these messages to the point of feeling inadequate, because we don't satisfy these images of success. We would all be better off if we didn't see these advertisements.

> *"Few rich men own their property. Their property owns them."*
>
> *- Robert G. Ingersoll*

Underarms that smell like wild roses and automatic climate controls in automobiles certainly aren't the keys to happiness. Consumerism relies on you being in constant discontentment. The next purchase is supposed to make you happy, but how could it? That would mean that you wouldn't purchase anything else if you attained happiness. Consequently, the satisfaction from any purchase is virtually always short-lived, and leads to the yearning for something else. Enough is never enough.

How More Money Can Add To Our Problems

Reuters news service in April, 1995 reported that the Bishop of Liverpool called for the government of England to review the concept of lotteries. If nothing else, he suggested that the prizes should be smaller. This was his response after a man in Liverpool committed suicide when he thought that he missed out on a lottery win worth the equivalent of about 13,000,000 U.S. dollars. Timothy O'Brien, 51 and a father of two children, shot himself after he failed to renew his weekly bet in a lottery on which he had bet the same numbers for over a year. O'Brien figured that he had missed out on the good life after these same numbers were apparently drawn the week he missed placing his bet.

Timothy O'Brien didn't realize that his life may not have changed for the better had he won. Many lottery winners wind up worse off after the big win due to the unexpected problems that accompany having a great deal of money. It is certain the big win wouldn't have brought him happiness, in light of his being the type of individual to commit suicide because of what might have been. It is also almost certain O'Brien would have had many more problems with a big win, than without one. Incidentally, at O'Brien's inquest it was discovered that he actually would have won only about 100 U.S. dollars.

> "If I keep my good character, I shall be rich enough."
>
> - Platonicus

Because of the false expectations that we place on being rich, attaining a great deal of money has disoriented many people like Timothy O'Brien. People often say things such as:

* If I had a lot of money, then I would be happy.
* If I had a lot of money, then I could enjoy my leisure time.
* If I had a lot of money, then I would feel good about myself.
* If I had a lot of money, more people would like me and then I could find a marriage partner.

If you have any of these thoughts, you are ruled by money and fear. You think that security means having a lot of money. This isn't true. If you believe money is synonymous with security, you won't be happy with a modest amount of money with which many genuinely secure people can be extremely happy. With a modest amount, you will be afraid that you don't have enough to take care of yourself. If you acquire a lot of money, you won't be happy because you will be afraid of losing it. The more money you get, the more afraid you will

"I sure wish I could afford a Porsche so I could impress women and take some of them out to dinner."

"Sometimes I wish I hadn't bought this Porsche so that I could afford to take out some women to dinner."

be of losing it.

An extensive study conducted in 1993 by Ed Diener, a University of Illinois psychologist, confirmed that more money than is needed for basic necessities can't buy happiness or solve problems. In fact, people end up with more problems when they end up with a lot of money. "As you start meeting basic needs, increases in income become less and less important," says Diener. People who receive a pay increase may be happier for a short time, but once they get used to the increase, they set their sights on more and more money so they can fulfil their new expectations. They want bigger houses, fancier cars, and more exotic vacations. These don't provide long-term happiness.

Extra income creates negative effects when people have more money than they need for basic needs and desires. Here are some of them:

* Relationships with friends and acquaintances suffer
* Keeping track of one's financial situation becomes more troublesome and time consuming
* Life in general becomes more complicated
* Fear of theft of property and money becomes more acute as people acquire more money
* Fear of losing money in investments increases

So, put money in its proper place. Discontent due to your perceived deprivation may be robbing you of a really good life. You may already have a good life, but you may fail to appreciate it. More money isn't the answer to happiness if your basic needs of food, water, shelter, and clothing are being met. Comparing yourself to others, who have more than you, will result in discontentment. You will always be able to find someone better off than you. The game of keeping up with the Joneses will result in a game of keeping up with the Smiths, if you ever surpass the Joneses.

> *"The only thing wealth does for some people is to make them worry about losing it."*
>
> *- Comte de Rivarol*

Even for many lower-income singles, a little bit of creativity and sacrifice can go a long way towards resolving financial problems. My sister, who is a single parent with two young children, doesn't make a great deal of money. Although her income isn't much more than the level designated as the poverty line for a parent with two children, she lives quite well. She doesn't try to maintain a higher lifestyle than she can afford; she doesn't think it is necessary for the kids. Having a nice car, a big house, and the latest fashions aren't necessary for a happy family. She knows once basic needs of food, water, clothing, and shelter are provided, children more than anything need a good education, emotional support, and love.

Wise people tell us that money won't solve all our problems. Many people ignore this wisdom and try to be rich regardless of the required sacrifices. They cling to the belief that money will bring them happiness. In many cases, people also want a lot of money because they think it will bring them power. Of course, people who don't know how to use power end up doing many things that are self-destructive.

The myth of money is manifested by the many people who are wealthy in material goods, but poor in spirit. Although they have a lot of money, they are poverty conscious. They don't know how to spend and enjoy their money. They also don't know how to share their resources with others less fortunate. In North America, the act of giving to the poor is done more by the poor than the rich.

Achieving the goal of making a lot of money won't make you happy. Self-fulfillment can't be found in material goods and a large bank account. A higher purpose in life will help you be happy. The higher purpose may help you make more money, but it doesn't matter much if it does. With a higher purpose in your life, you will be happy with either a modest amount or a great deal of money.

> *"When life's problems seem overwhelming, look around and see what other people are coping with. You may consider yourself fortunate."*
>
> *- Ann Landers*

Appreciate What You Have And Grow Rich

After his father died in 1971, Jean-Claude (Baby Doc) Duvalier inherited the duty of ruling Haiti. Forced out of office in 1986 by the citizens of Haiti, Baby Doc and his wife Michele weren't content with having stuffed a Air Haiti cargo airplane with a lot of loot. As they were being flown out of Haiti on a US Air Force airplane, they bumped Michele's grandparents along with nine other passengers off the airplane, so they could take more loot. Baby Doc and Michele escaped to the French Riviera where they led the good life, spending millions of dollars a year. Baby Doc and his wife divorced in 1990. While single, Baby Doc squandered all his fortune and was recently evicted from his luxury villa.

It seems that people like Baby Doc will have money problems regardless of how much money they acquire. Attaining a proper balance isn't the easiest thing in the world. In North America, more money is the common denominator for acquiring material comfort and achieving social status. Brainwashed that having more material goods means a better life, people gradually and quite willingly end up with financial commitments and responsibilities, which are easy to get into and difficult to eliminate. The mistake which many people make is trying to maintain a particular lifestyle when they can't afford it.

> *"To be handed a lot of money is to be handed a glass sword, blade first. Best handle it very carefully, sir, very slowly while you puzzle what it's for."*
>
> *- Richard Bach, Bridge Across Forever*

If you have financial problems, then you must deal with them creatively. As with most problems, financial problems have to be put into proper perspective. For example, if you are in serious debt, collection agents will intimidate you only if you allow them. In North America, you aren't going to be put in jail because you owe a lot of money. When I was living on the poverty line, and had a collection agency hounding me for a loan, I had a number of creative tricks up my sleeve to deal with the agent. My ace-in-the-hole solution was to avoid saying anything more once the agent identified himself as Mr. Harrison on the telephone. Instead, I just banged the receiver against the desk until he hung up. It didn't take long for the collection agency to return the account back to the lending institution. When I was in a position to pay back the institution, I started making payments on my terms, without having to deal with an obnoxious collection agent.

Now is the time to pass on the secret of the two powerful ways to handle money, which are equally effective. The first powerful way is to spend less than you earn. If you have tried this, and it hasn't worked, the second one is definitely for you. The second powerful way is to earn more than you spend. That's all there is to the money game - use only one of these powerful principles and you have handled money.

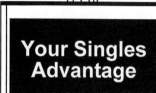

Your Singles Advantage

- **You can blow the money on a Porsche instead of a house**
- **You can use all the hot water**
- **You can take more vacations**

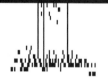

If you never have enough money regardless of how much you make, you are probably squandering money on things that you don't need. Finding out why you are a spendthrift living on the edge is important. You must spend some time learning how to handle money. Handling money properly will make you realize that cutting back on your lifestyle and expenses won't make you feel deprived. Try downscaling your spending habits - you will be amazed by how little you actually need.

On the other extreme of squanderers who misspend are the misers who can't spend. They can't enjoy their money regardless of how much they have. If you are one of these people, you are suffering from a disease. You must accept that there is only one reason for having money; the ultimate purpose for money is to spend it. What is the point of having money in abundance if you haven't learned how to spend it? The ability to enjoy your prosperity is essential for fulfillment from what money has to offer. Dream up some creative and fun ways to spend some of your money. If after some time you haven't

> *"After spending some money in his sleep, Hermon the miser was so hopping mad he hanged himself."*
>
> *- Lucilius*

been able to come up with some good ideas, give me a call. I'll have no problem with helping you spend your money - no amount will be too big for me! I will come up with some fascinating spending ideas that will liberate you from your misery.

> *"Ninety percent of my money I intend to spend on wild women, booze, and good times and the other ten percent I will spend foolishly."*
>
> *- Tug McGraw*

Putting money in its place means that you realize more doesn't mean merrier. Defining your well-being and identity in terms of material possessions and your bank account isn't going to bring you long-term satisfaction. Working hard just for the sake of making a lot of money is an act of desperation. Whether happiness or money, if you chase after it, you are likely to drive it away from yourself. As stated in Chapter 4, once you stop being obsessed with making a lot of money, and instead start doing what you enjoy, you will be rewarded immensely with the satisfaction and enjoyment that you get out of your work. Paradoxically, a great deal of money may also be one of your rewards once you stop being obsessed with money.

Money should reflect your creative energy and inner security. Using your creative energy while working at a job with a higher purpose will bring the money that you need to lead an abundant life. The more willing you are to risk and follow your inner calling in life, the more money you will attract in the long term. You will also need less money to be happy because your self-fulfillment will come from pursuing your personal mission. Earning a lot of money from your work is just a bonus. Although you can do without this bonus, you can also celebrate when it does come.

Keep in mind that focusing too much on having lots of money will detract from the other important elements of life. Money can't buy intimacy or genuine friendships. Attempting to use money to buy love and acceptance will only lead to superficial friendships and eventual dejection. Close friendships are based on mutual respect and don't cost any money at all. Keeping desires at a minimum can actually provide for a happier life. Learning to appreciate what you have is the way to a rich life.

> *"Jesus, please teach me to appreciate what I have before time forces me to appreciate what I had."*
>
> *- Susan L. Lenzkes*

9. Tips For The Romantically Challenged

The Dating Dilemma

Help, I need somebody.
Help, not just anybody.
Help, you know I need someone.
Help!

Meeting someone special and forming an intimate, loving relationship is still the dream of most unattached singles. It is natural for singles to long for a significant relationship with someone. Most singles would choose to be married if they were able to create a meaningful relationship with someone they love. Meeting and connecting with other singles isn't necessarily easy. The dating dilemma exists for many singles out there; the dilemma is one of being able to live happily single, and at the same time, being able to meet people so they can share themselves with others. Dating in the 1990s is somewhat different than it was in the recent past. In fact, compared to the 1950s and 1960s, dating has changed significantly.

> *"I don't think of myself as single. I'm romantically challenged."*
>
> *- Stephanie H. Piro*

To some people, the dating game is an adventure; to others, the dating game is tedious and filled with anxiety. Some singles consider dating such a chore that they may wind up in marriages of the less-than-satisfactory variety, due to their haste in getting married.

"My name is Howard. How do you like me so far?"

"So far, I think that I probably like you more than spiders and flat tires."

How can singles meet other compatible singles? Winning at the dating game is a consuming passion for most singles. It is a complex game; meeting someone appears to have become harder with time. In 1993, 19 percent of women had never married, whereas in 1970, six percent hadn't. The percentage of never-married men in 1993 was 30, and in 1970, it was only nine. Yet, studies indicate that 72 percent of single women and 56 percent of single men would like to get married in the next year.

Single parents have all the hassles other singles have with dating, and then some. Single men and women with children will have more difficulty in dating, because of time pressures and the constraints that children impose. After taking care of the children, little time is left for socializing. In general, the opportunities are fewer in number for single parents, because they can't date as often.

Women in certain cities may have an especially hard time meeting people. A recent study done by Harvard and Yale indicated that marriage for a college-educated single white woman, who reaches the age of 30, is extremely unlikely. Indeed, *Newsweek* magazine played on the Harvard-Yale study to say that the chances of a 40-year-old woman marrying were as good (or bad) as being shot by a terrorist.

"Burt Reynolds once asked me out. I was in his room."

- Phyllis Diller

Due to the difficulty that many singles have in meeting others, the matching industry is booming in North America. Those searching for Mr. Right or Ms. Right can use the services of health spas, singles clubs, dating services, newspaper ads, books, sports organizations, dining clubs, cruise lines, Club Med, and counselors. Many types of support groups exist such as SINBADS, which stands for "Women who are: Single In Need of Blokes, in Absolutely Desperate State." Another support group is U.S.W.I.S.O.M.W.A.G.M.O.H.O.T.M., which stands for "United Single Women in Search Of Men Who Aren't Gay, Married, Or Hung-up On Their Mothers."

To Be Involved Means To Complicate Or Make Difficult

In the 1990s, you have to be more aware and creative to win at the dating game than ever before. If you want to enter a relationship with substance, the price you will have to pay is your freedom. In some way, your individuality will have to be compromised. Be sure that you are prepared for a relationship before you decide to look for one. If you are recently separated or divorced, the time may not be right. Some individuals require a lengthy period before getting involved again; others desire a new relationship as soon as possible.

You must be careful that you haven't fallen into the unbreakable trap of living solely for yourself. Connecting with someone else means that you will have to make compromises. Focusing too much on your own needs and schedule can turn off other people. There will have to be some commitment to another person and his or her schedule, if you want to connect in a relationship. Becoming too set in your own ways can make you too structured and reserved to allow someone special into your own space.

Before you strive for an intimate, committed relationship, ensure that you have put relationships in a reality-based perspective - instead of a Harlequin-romance-based perspective. Elements of relationships can include wild beginnings, friendship, love, disagreements, crises, children, boredom, and endings. However, not every relationship will result in true love and long-term commitments.

> *"Give me my golf clubs, fresh air and a beautiful partner, and you can keep my golf clubs and the fresh air."*
>
> *- Jack Benny*

Relationships are characterized by intimacy, attachment, and involvement. The question is: Do you want to get involved in a relationship? If you said yes, there is something important you must

Your Singles Advantage

- **You can have as many weird friends stay over as you would like**
- **You don't have to share the 16-inch pizza you made**

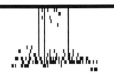

consider: The common dictionary definition of involvement is "to complicate or make difficult." Most people are literally involved in relationships; life has become complicated and difficult - due to their involvement.

As a result of the myriad of difficulties and complications, people are trying to make relationships and marriages "work." Thomas Moore in his book *"Soul Mates"* theorizes that we are wasting our time trying to make relationships work. The goal of making relationships work is based on the ideal or perfect model. And if you are older than sixteen, you should have learned by now that perfection is unattainable.

A relationship is going to take time, effort, and energy. Relationships lead to both pleasure and pain; total failure is also a possibility. Relationships enrich our souls at the same time that they complicate our lives. Moore says: "Relationships have a way of rubbing our nose in the slime of life - an experience we would rather forego, but one that offers an important exposure to our own depth."

Despite the potential complications, you may want to be in a relationship for the positive reasons of intimacy, love, support, great communication, wonderful sex - and a hundred more. If so, then you must do what is necessary to create one. The next time you are feeling sorry for yourself because you haven't connected with that special person, recall this is going to take time and effort. There are many people out there right now doing the things that are necessary to meet someone. You have to do the same.

Looking For Mr. Or Ms. Right

When looking for Mr. Right or Ms. Right, most singles are looking for an ideal partner. Potential dating partners are supposed to be bearers of all the traits that our ideal marriage partner would have. A good way to undermine your chances for a meaningful relationship is to try to find someone who is going to live up to your parents' expectations, rather than your own, of the marriage partner you should have. Disregard most of what relatives and friends think about someone who interests you. It is none of their business if you choose someone who doesn't meet their expectations. Also, if you want a meaningful relationship, avoid the dull compromise where you settle for somebody who is less than satisfactory.

You are undermining your chances for a meaningful relationship by looking for someone who will give you everything you desire in a partner. No one can ever give you 100 percent of what a perfect marriage partner could offer. You are also undermining your chances for a meaningful relationship if you select a partner for the following functions:

> *"Better that a girl have beauty than brains because boys see better than they think."*
>
> *- Unknown Wise Person*

An Authentic Partner Is NOT:

* Someone who is supposed to have exactly the same interests as you
* Someone you can control
* Someone you can totally rely on for financial support
* Someone who is totally dependent on you financially
* Someone who is a saviour or a protector
* Someone who is largely dependent on you emotionally
* Someone to clean up after you
* Someone to cook your meals
* Someone who can provide you with unlimited, adventurous sex that makes your eyes pop out every night
* Someone to mow lawns and fix washing machines
* Someone who agrees with you all the time
* Someone who drops their goals in favor of yours
* Someone who is supposed to be extroverted to compensate for your shyness
* Someone who totally eliminates other satisfying relationships with friends and family for your sake
* Someone who is supposed to be self-directed and highly goal oriented to provide direction in your messy life
* Someone who will compensate for the characteristics which you lack in your personality

Your prospective marriage partner may have elements of some of these functions, and should have little or nothing to do with most of them. If you need someone for the main purpose of cleaning up your mess, then hire yourself a maid. Similarly, if you need someone for the main purpose of fixing the washing machine or the stove, then hire the Maytag man. Should any one of the above become the sole function of your marriage partner, then you probably haven't found, and won't find, "the real thing."

When you are looking for a partner, recall that negative and needy people can seriously disrupt your life. Try to avoid going out with anyone who has more problems than you. You certainly don't want to go out with someone who carries more baggage than a Boeing 747. You will end up having to carry some, or most, of this excess baggage. There's a price to pay for traveling with excess baggage on the airlines, and there's a big price to pay for traveling with excess baggage in your life. If you choose to go out with someone who has the mentality of an ax murderer, don't expect intellectual conversations and dining at fine restaurants.

> *"If people waited to know each other before they were married, the world wouldn't be so grossly over-populated."*
>
> *- W. Somerset Maugham*

In an authentic relationship, there is an absence of need or dependency. Each partner is ultimately responsible for his or her own happiness. The partners care about each other, but neither partner feels an obligation to obsessively and totally take care of the other individual. Both individuals may keep developing their own identities, interests, goals, and friends in an authentic intimate relationship. The relationship is also characterized by many shared interests, common values, mutual friends, good communication, and regular compromises. If we haven't found "the real thing," where have we gone wrong? Back to Ralph Waldo Emerson who said: "The only way to have a friend, is to be one." The only way to find an authentic mate is to be one.

Exciting People Are More Trouble Than They Are Worth

If you are bored, and think that meeting someone exciting may be the answer to your problems, it's worth noting that certain exciting singles are more trouble than they are worth. Exciting marriage partners may also be individuals who are the most easily bored.

Some people, who appear to be leading exciting lives, are pursuing adventure because they are addicted to novelty. Psychologist Marvin Zuckerman found that, although most men and women shun novelty, a small minority - known as thrill seekers - thrive on it.

Thrill seekers are obsessed with experiencing adventure and variety in everything they undertake. They appear to be immune to boredom, since they lead exciting lives. Paradoxically, sensation seekers are more susceptible to boredom than the rest of the population. Everyday life often becomes too predictable and boring for them.

Zuckerman placed thrill seekers in four classifications: The first group crave activities and outdoor sports which feature speed and danger. Making up the second group are those individuals who seek inner experiences through drugs, alcohol, travel, and avant-garde lifestyles. Swingers, the third group, drink alcohol, gamble, and go for sexual variety and wild parties. Members of the fourth group are the hardest to satisfy because they can't tolerate predictable individuals and any routine.

Thrill seekers are high risk takers. They may have great difficulty in extracting meaning and purpose from everyday life. These high risk takers are normally impulsive and uninhibited. They favor friends with offbeat lifestyles. Sports, such as sky diving and mountain climbing, are preferred over jogging or tennis. The addiction to stimulation may also influence thrill seekers to gamble excessively, commit crimes, and abuse drugs.

> *"Many a man has fallen in love with a girl in a light so dim he would not have chosen a suit by it."*
>
> *- Maurice Chevalier*

Being involved with a thrill seeker to ease your own boredom can be risky indeed, especially if you are looking for a long-term relationship. A relationship between a high-sensation seeker and a low-sensation seeker has a lower probability of survival than a normal relationship. A well-adjusted individual, who tolerates routine well, tends to bore and irritate a thrill seeker in the long term. Long-term relationships are difficult for many thrill seekers, unless the relationship is constantly exciting and filled with novelty. They are easily bored in most relationships; this can influence them to pursue affairs. Chances for a successful relationship with a thrill seeker will be increased if you are also a thrill seeker.

Does Rejection Make You Say The "F" Word?

While searching for a relationship, the majority of singles are likely to experience a measure of rejection. There will always be risk involved in the search for love. Fear of rejection can immobilize people so they don't put any effort into meeting others. Due to the risk of rejection, some people choose not to get involved at all.

People tend to want to use the "F" word when discussing their rejection by others. "Failure" is the "F" word I am talking about, which to many people signifies a condition almost as bad as some types of terminal cancer. The fear of failure or rejection goes hand in hand with low self-esteem. Supposedly, rejection is a case of serious failure, a condition from which one doesn't recover.

It is okay to view rejection as failure, provided the failure is viewed as a positive experience. Failure - lots of it - is a prerequisite for success in life. Viewed from a positive perspective, failure is a transforming experience. Successful people know how important it is to be able to handle and celebrate failure, because their most important projects in life have required a lot of failure before success was achieved. To them, failures are nothing more - or less for that matter - than big steps towards success and greatness.

"I Gave Her a Ring, and She Gave Me the Finger."

- Words in a country song

Asking someone out on a date offers the opportunity to get to know someone wonderful, but it offers the chance of being rejected by someone wonderful. Singles looking to meet others have to risk rejection; they are undermining their chances for a relationship if they are afraid of being rejected. The ability to take risks is important in all aspects of life. There is always a risk of failure or rejection in running for political office, going to a job interview, investing in a business, confronting a friend about a sensitive issue, and asking someone for a date. Even once singles meet someone, and get immersed in relationships, failure is still a possibility since most relationships don't last forever.

Danielle Steel, an accomplished author of several best-selling books, was somewhat of a failure in her early jump into married life. In her words, the theme of Steel's first book was: "Every woman falls

in love with a bastard at least once in her life."
Danny Zugelder, her second husband, is now
serving 40 years in prison. Her first husband was
convicted for bank robbery, and later for rape. Bill
Toth, her third husband, is an unemployed
recovering drug addict who was convicted of
many petty crimes committed to support his
addiction. Steel's latest marriage to John Traina is reported to be in
great condition.

"If the phone doesn't ring, it's me."

- Song by Jimmy Buffet

Every time you go out and reveal yourself where there are
people, you risk success and failure. You have to risk failure if you
want to meet others, and possibly your spouse-to-be. Some of the
dates will go great, and some will be disappointments. You can get
rejected at any stage in a relationship. When rejection strikes, just
chalk it up to the person not knowing the true you. A few incidents of
rejection just represents a few more steps to acceptance. Don't take
the rejection personally; we all get rejected.

Although rejection is awkward,
uncomfortable, and inconvenient, it isn't the
end of the world. Rejection works both ways;
people have a right to reject you as much as
you have a right to reject others. You get to
reject other people, and potentially create the
same effect on other people, as people who
reject you have on you. Note that I said
"potentially" create the same effect.
Well-balanced people won't get dejected
because of a little rejection here and there. It
isn't the event of rejection that does
emotional damage to us as much as how we
react to the event. We are the ones who
choose the effect that rejection will ultimately
have on us.

Your Singles Advantage

- **You don't need to hide old love letters**
- **You get to open or close the windows without objection**

Just as failure - a lot of it - is often
necessary to attain success at anything
important, rejection - a lot of it - is necessary
to attain acceptance by someone important.
Many of the people in relationships today

have been rejected dozens, and even hundreds, of times, before they established their present relationships. There is no way to avoid the possibility of rejection if you want to have a chance at meeting the right partner or soulmate.

If you have recently struck out with someone, then remember the words of Winston Churchill: "Never, never, never, never give up!" Rejection is part of the dating game; we all get rejected if we choose to play the game. Remember that you are trying to find that one person - not ten or twenty. With almost six billion people on this earth, there are still a lot of individuals to check out.

To Be Interesting, Be Interested

Contact with others is important if you want to meet someone for a long-term, committed relationship. The conditions that enhance your chances of meeting a lover can be created. Waiting and being patient for someone special to appear is the wise thing to do, but you can't do it at home. You have to go out and wait and be patient in the company of people. Make it happen by reaching out; let people get to know the real you.

When you spot someone who interests you, learn to give of yourself. Be interested rather than interesting. By being interested in him or her, you are making that person feel special. If you put all your energies into being interesting, you will end up doing what most people are doing - trying to be interesting. The problem is that everyone else is standing around trying to be interesting, and wondering why no one is finding them interesting. Instead, if you risk and go up to someone and show an interest in him or her, you are immediately more interesting. In other words, the best way to be interesting to others is to be interested in them. You must take the chance by making the first move. Communicate your interest and you may end up being interesting, because you have created the opportunity to exchange ideas, likes, dislikes, values, and feelings.

"Give what you have. To someone, it may be better than you dare to think."

- Henry Wadsworth Longfellow

If you are disappointed that nothing is happening in your life, you certainly can't sit at home watching television, and expect to be discovered. Waiting to be discovered is just another one of those windfall-from-nowhere states of mind. If you would rather stay at home on a Saturday night - watching some TV program that is going to do nothing more for you than lower your IQ and put on some weight - then don't complain that you don't have anyone in your life. You are going to have to pay the price with courage and effort. This shouldn't be a surprise; there is no substitute for conscious effort. That special someone isn't going to wind up on your doorstep looking for you.

Even beautiful women (and handsome men) can't wait around to be discovered. Many have the problem of not being asked out. In an article, *"Where are men? Joan moans,"* written by Marilyn Beck and Stacy Jenel Smith (carried in the February 5, 1995 issue of the *Vancouver Province*), Joan Lunden, co-host of *Good Morning, America* is reported to have said: "It was three years ago this month that I moved out of the house. Since then, I've only had a few dates and, believe me, that hasn't been my choice." Lunden was reported to have a hard time finding a man in her life since her separation from her former husband Michael Krauss. She seemed to blame her lack of romance on men being intimidated by beautiful women. Lunden claimed several of her beautiful women friends had the same problem. Although she wasn't saying her life was unexciting, she did state: "It's not that my life isn't exciting. It's just that I'd like to share it with someone."

> *"There's a difference between beauty and charm. A beautiful woman is one I notice. A charming woman is one who notices me."*
>
> *- John Erskine*

Regardless of how beautiful they are, women should be asking men for dates, if they aren't getting all the dates that they would like. The problem I find with many women who stand for liberation is that they don't really mean it. They mean "selective liberation," a type of liberation which benefits them in certain ways, but doesn't inconvenience them, or make life uncomfortable in other ways. Despite all the books they have read on liberation, they are still waiting for Prince Charming to come riding on his horse to save them. I tell my women friends that if they are truly liberated and have high self-esteem, they shouldn't have any inhibitions about asking men out. Of course, they are going to get turned down occasionally, regardless of how beautiful they are. It is about time they had to deal with having to build up the courage to ask men out, and then deal with the rejection that men have had to deal with.

Women should not only ask men for dates - they should pay if they do. I don't enjoy overpowering women, but I have certainly been asked out by women and accepted many times. Below is an example of an invitation which I received from a woman:

> *"Please feel free to call me the next time you are in Vancouver. Perhaps I can treat you to coffee / lunch / drinks / dinner, or any combination of the above. I am looking forward to hearing from you."*

This is the last paragraph from the letter written by the woman who took a sabbatical (mentioned on page 103). I found this woman's invitation pleasantly assertive, but not overpowering. Because she was interested in me, I found her interesting.

When you are meeting people, the key is not to be desperate. The least amount of respect and affection are going to flow your way when you seek it the most. It is unlikely that you will meet someone special if you are desperate for that relationship with Mr. or Ms. Right. Most people can easily spot any hint of desperation. If you are desperate for a relationship, you are more than likely to meet Mr. or Ms. Wrong who preys on needy people.

"The main difference between men and women is that men are lunatics and women are idiots."

- Dame Rebecca West, British novelist

When you are happy being single, you will radiate a sense of self-confidence. Your self-confidence will attract others who are self-confident and happy. These are the qualities you should be looking for in that special person you want to meet.

Also don't "appear" to be needy or desperate. You can appear desperate, even if you aren't. Here is a case in point: When I go on the first dinner date with a new, interesting woman and she asks me about my marriage plans - even before the waiter has taken our order - I immediately wonder if I have just blown 70 dollars. (On the odd occasion, when she is paying, I still may have lost an hour or two of my time). Having dinner with someone who appears desperate to get married isn't to my taste. I know that I shouldn't be surprised at the

138

number of women who ask about marriage. A recent survey indicated that 42 percent of women talk about marriage and kids on the first date. Nonetheless, I immediately am looking for more signs of desperation when a woman asks me about marriage so early in the dating game. Personally, I prefer to go out with some of the other 58 percent of women who don't appear to be desperate.

Learn to relax, enjoy yourself, and be yourself when meeting others. Most singles state that they enjoy being single most when they aren't actively or desperately seeking a dating partner. Rarely do people meet that special person at the time they think they will. Many men and women reveal that special person entered their lives when they least expected it, and when they weren't desperately searching for someone.

Physical attraction is important in meeting other singles. We all go for attractiveness in potential marriage partners; it is a matter of degree. Style is just as important as attractiveness. Don't dress like a slob. The day you look like a major contender for the least-likely-to-succeed contest is the day you will run into a prospective date, who is working alone waiting for someone to chat with. If he or she thinks that your tacky black coat signifies there is likely a 1983 Peugot in town with its black seat covers missing, he or she isn't likely to be too interested in you.

> *"I'm tired of all this nonsense about beauty being only skin deep. That's deep enough. What do you want, an adorable pancreas?"*
>
> *- Jean Kerr*

Dress well, but don't overdress. Being a slave to fashion can turn off many people if they think you are more into superficial elements than the meaningful ones. You may end up looking desperate or too well-off for others. Nonetheless, the reality is that looking good and being well-dressed do matter to most people. Although in-tune individuals are watching for other more important qualities besides good looks, they still prefer others who look good and are well-dressed.

Self-confidence is extremely important. You can't go around looking like you have taken every available course on how to be dysfunctional. When you have an aura of self-confidence, you will attract people much faster. The ability to be yourself will attract people with the least effort on your behalf. Forget about putting on a mask; Halloween is for kids, and should only be celebrated once a year. Trying to impress others, by pretending to be someone you would like to be, instead of who you truly are, will backfire. You have heard this before, but it is worth repeating: The best way to impress someone of great quality is not to try to impress them.

"A man who was loved by 300 women singled me out to live with him. Why? I was the only one without a cat."

- Elayne Boosler

If you are an in-tune person operating with excellence in mind, you will undoubtedly be looking for someone who is also in tune. That person will be self-confident, self-reliant, and relaxed. He or she will have a purpose and know what he or she wants out of life. You are seeking someone with an abundance of self-esteem who will light a fire inside you.

How To Bore And Turn Off Other People

Try to be charismatic when meeting new people. Coming across appearing boring can be detrimental to further meetings - first impressions are important! An article in the November, 1988 issue of *Personality and Social Psychology* cites researchers, Mark Leary, assistant psychology professor at Wake Forest University, and Harry Reis, psychology professor at the University of Rochester in New York, who established a boring index to determine which behaviors were deemed more boring than others. There are several behaviors that others find boring: trying to be funny to impress others, going off on tangents, talking about trivial or superficial things, overusing small talk or slang, complaining about oneself, trying to be nice to be liked by others, and showing no interest in others.

All of the above behaviors tend to bore most people. Some of these behaviors are more boring than others. Reis and Leary found that the most boring behaviors were talking about trivial or superficial things and showing no interest in others. The least boring behaviors were trying to be nice and trying to be funny. People, who complain about themselves and utter trivialities, are more boring than people who overuse slang or try too hard to be nice.

You may be undermining your opportunities for dates if you are boring, do weird things, or conduct yourself in ways that are questionable to others. Here are some traits and behaviors which can cause people to look at you as doubtful dating material:

You May Be Boring Or Questionable Dating Material If:

* Your idea of quality time is spending an hour or two talking to your horse and drinking a few cans of no-name beer
* You have more than one picture or statue of Ralph Klein or Newt Gingrich in your living room
* Your idea of luxury accommodation is sleeping in the backseat of an abandoned Mecedes-Benz
* You can't figure out why someone who is strong, big, and husky is a member of a men's support group
* You belong to a fitness club where half of the members own pit bulls and the other half wish they did
* You love your car, your stereo, your dog, your cat, or your pet snake more than you could ever love a marriage partner
* Your idea of a wild Saturday night is taking a loop on the ring bus and then hanging around the laundromat for a while
* Your favorite T-shirt says: "I like sex, watching TV, and drinking beer."
* You drive around with more than one flat tire
* You have been divorced three times and you are only 25
* Your car is so rusted out that you throw beer bottles outside without having to roll down the windows
* Regardless of which of your three sweaters you wear, someone is always saying something like "How long do you have to wear that sweater before you win the bet?"
* Your idea of a gourmet meal is a heated TV dinner with two or three cans of no-name beer
* Your favorite activity is heading down to an after-hours nightclub on fetish night to take part in the public spankings
* You use the "F" word more than four times in a ten-word sentence
* You brag about how well-educated you are because you took three years of grade nine

Your image may suffer if any of the above describe you. Whether you are boring or questionable dating material will depend on how many people say you are. Here is a good way to tell whether you are what someone says you are. If you

> "His mother should have thrown him away and kept the stork."
>
> - Mae West

encounter twenty people in a day, and one calls you a horse, don't worry about it. If you encounter twenty people in a day, and two people call you a horse, you still don't have too much about which to be concerned. However, if you encounter twenty people in a day, and seventeen or more call you a horse, then you should immediately get yourself a saddle and start eating hay! Of course, the other alternative is to stop being a horse.

"If you're given a choice between money and sex appeal - take the money. As you get older, the money will become your sex appeal."

- Katharine Hepburn

If you have negative charisma, and are the life of the party only when you leave, you must do something about your personality. You must pay the price needed to correct the deficiencies. Psychologists confirm that charismatic people aren't born with their charisma. The special charm that attracts others like a magnet and energizes them can be learned. What you must do is develop an inner radiance, and project a love of life outward when you are with people. Charisma is displayed when you have high self-esteem; it reflects itself in your high positive energy and joie de vivre.

Breaking The Ice

In her memoirs, Elizabeth Taylor recalled her first meeting with Richard Burton on the set during the making of Cleopatra in Rome in 1962. She stated: "He sort of sidled over to me and said, 'Has anybody ever told you that you're a very pretty girl?' and I said to myself, Oy gevaldt, here's the great lover, the great wit, the great intellectual of Wales, and he comes up with a line like that." Despite her disappointment with Burton's icebreaker, chemistry prevailed; Taylor and Burton got married - not only once, but twice.

Which kinds of icebreakers work best when trying to meet someone? It depends on the person. The academic journal *Sex Roles* cited a 1986 study called *Preference for Opening Lines: Comparing Ratings by Men*

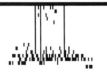

Your Singles Advantage

- **Your favorite, most expensive clothes don't get shrunk in the dryer when he or she "helps" with the laundry**

and Women which rated opening lines used by men and women trying to meet members of the opposite sex. Of the three categories of icebreakers identified - cute, innocuous, and direct - the study found that the cute-flippant opening lines were least desirable. Women disliked the cute-flippant opening lines more so than men. According to the study, "What do you think of the band?" will work a lot better in a night club than "You're undoubtedly wondering what a nice guy like me is doing in a place like this." Also on the hit list are "Is that really your hair?" and "You remind me of someone I used to date."

> Bookstore pickup line:
>
> *"Have you seen a copy of Tax Tips for Billionaires?"*
>
> *- From David Letterman*

The best opening lines are either compliments or sincere questions. Compliments, such as "I think you look great in that suit," and questions, such as "Have you been here before?", work best because they are likely to get a response. How you say the icebreaker is just as important as what you say. The tone of voice will send signals as to whether you are flirting due to sexual interest, or just making conversation to kill time until someone more interesting comes along.

Using any icebreaker sets you up for the risk of rejection. If you are a risk taker and want to use cute-flippant lines, here are a few for you to try: (Report back to me if any of these is especially effective since I may want to use it as well).

* I seem to have lost my phone number. Do you think I could borrow yours?
* You must be tired because you have been running through my mind all day.
* I don't dance but I'd love to hold you while you do.
* I think you are cuter than a speckled pup.
* Do you want Ms. Right or Ms. Right-Now?
* Would you like to come over to my place and see my rock collection?
* Excuse me, but I don't believe we have met. I am Mr. Right.
* Let's get together later. We can do things the king and queen haven't even thought of.

Your first conversation in the courting game is crucial; it could be your last. In the early stages, successful courting requires that you be patient and take your time. Being too aggressive will repel the other person. Talking too much, touching too soon, or appearing too desperate will lead to undesirable results. It is important to be relaxed and sincere.

Icebreakers are for women as well as for men. Contrary to popular beliefs the world over, researchers have found women in most societies, including North American society, initiate the courting ritual at least 50 percent of the time. In fact, North America women coax potential lovers into conversations 67 percent of the time by initiating conversations with jokes, compliments, and questions. Males aren't as conscious as women of the signals - verbal or non-verbal - that are used to initiate flirtation. Men are also slower to respond. Experts on love signals believe that if men would learn to read the verbal and non-verbal flirtatious signals women give them, there would be fewer single and lonely men.

Looking For The Strong Solvent Type

As with beauty and attractiveness, money and social position play a big part in the dating game. It is reasonable to assume that with more women earning respectable wages, and acquiring higher financial and independently-earned social status, fewer women would be concerned about men's financial and social status. This reasonable assumption is wrong! Studies have shown that women, regardless of how much income they command, have a tendency to place greater emphasis than men on a partner's financial status, Some psychologists claim this tendency is genetic.

> *"The most popular labor-saving device today is still a husband with money."*
>
> *- Joey Adams, Cindy and I*

A 1989 study by David Buss found that in every culture of 37 studied, women placed much more emphasis on a potential spouse's financial prospects and/or social status. Men tend to choose a healthy looking companion; women tend to choose a standard of living. Women are more bottom-line oriented when choosing a marriage partner.

In a 1995 study, psychology professor Robert Cramer, Ph.D. and his associates at Cal State, San Bernardino found that men selected attractiveness, youth, health, and sexual responsiveness as the most

144

important traits in an ideal partner. Women chose intelligence, motivation, honesty, and earning capacity. This study confirms women's complaints that men want young, beautiful women as marriage partners; it also confirms men's complaints that women are most interested in men with money. Why do men still seek the young and healthy, and women vote for financial security? Some behavioral scientists such as Cramer state that both interests are the product of biological drives to reproduce.

While browsing through the newspapers' singles advertisements, I find it interesting how many women searching for a man are looking for someone hard-working, professional, accomplished, successful, or financially secure. In other words, someone in a low-paying, low-status job need not apply. I have at times wondered where this leaves me - an author who works only four to five hours a day and writes books about the joys of not working. Now you know why I am not married.

Some men like to use their power and money to their advantage in the dating game. There are still many women who will be immediately interested in a male dentist who offers security, status, and a high standard of living, but will promptly discard the same man if he tells them that he works as a laborer at $7.50 an hour. Other men feel dehumanized when women evaluate them in terms of their status, power, and money (or lack of it). Evaluating men based on their job status and income is common among women, even those who earn earn high salaries. Many men feel just as cheapened by women who see them as "meal tickets" as women feel when men see them as "sex objects."

> *"I require only three things in a man: he must be handsome, ruthless and stupid."*
>
> *- Dorothy Parker*

The reality is economic standards are part of the dating game and marriage. Virtually all of us consider the financial status of prospective partners. You do it and I do it - it is a matter of degree. Nonetheless, when dating women, I will always remember Leslie Parish's and Richard Bach's comments about money made in Bach's book *"Bridge Across Forever."* In the true story of Bach's search for his soulmate, he relates how Leslie Parish, his friend at the time and not yet his lover, was giving him advice why he shouldn't be using money to try and win over the women he was dating. She stated: "You do what you think is right. But don't fool yourself that anybody's going to love you because you pay their rent or buy their groceries. One way to be sure they will not love you is to let them depend on you for money. I know what I'm talking about." After considering her advice, and thinking about the women he was seeing and showering with money and gifts, Bach agreed with Parrish. He replied: "It's not love. None of them love me. We enjoy each other. We're happy mutual parasites."

Do Dating Partners Get Better Or Worse With Age?

> *"How absurd and delicious it is to be in love with someone younger than yourself. Everyone should try it."*
>
> *- Barbara Pym*

Should singles consider the age difference when looking for a marriage partner? Men, more than women, place emphasis on the age of the prospective partner. According to some sociologists, the reason is men have a tendency to focus on the woman's ability to produce children. In his 1989 study, David Buss found males preferred younger marriage partners in all 37 countries that he surveyed. Although the tendency is for men to marry women about five to ten years younger, the age difference can be considerable either way. Here are a few examples of celebrity relationships with considerable age differences:

Women Who Had Younger Lovers

♥ After meeting Dinah Shore, when appearing on her show Dinah's Place, Burt Reynolds, 19 years her junior, spent most of his time attempting to convince her to go on a fling with him to Palm Springs. A long love affair ensued. When it broke up, Reynolds claimed Shore was "the great love of my life."

♥ Cher, 46 at the time, had a relationship with Rob Camilletti who was half her age. Cher wanted to marry him badly at one time, but he resisted, saying he needed time to find himself.

♥ Ayn Rand at the age of 55 started an affair with Nathaniel Branden, a protege, 25 at the time. The affair lasted 14 years, until Branden fell in love with a younger woman.

Men Who Had Younger Lovers

♥ In 1954, at the age of 64, Groucho Marx married Eden Hartford, a 24-year-old model. The marriage lasted 15 years.

♥ At 52, former Rolling Stone Bill Wyman married 18-year-old Mandy Smith. The marriage only lasted a few months. This story has more: In 1993, Stephen Wyman, the 33-year-old son of Bill, became engaged to Patsy Smith, the 46-year-old mother of Mandy.

♥ Charlie Chaplin at 54 married for the fourth time. His wife was 18-year-old Oona O'Neil, who was being courted by Chaplin's sons. O'Neil fell in love with the father. It was a happy marriage with Chaplin and O'Neil having eight children, the last being born when Chaplin was 73 and O'Neil was 37.

The chances of marriages lasting for women are best when they choose husbands two to ten years older than them according to a 1995 study by Statistics Canada. The study, based on six million married and divorced couples, indicates that couples with a small age difference are less likely to divorce than couples with a large one. The lowest divorce rate belongs to couples where the wife is six years younger than the husband. Chances for a divorce are much greater if a woman marries a younger man. Similarly, the chances for divorce increase considerably when a man is much older than his wife.

Many people are apparently unconcerned about the risks of dating and marrying when there is a big age difference. The Statistics Canada study found that in Canada (with a population one-tenth of the U.S.), there are at least 14 women with husbands 70 or more years younger than them, and 87 men with wives 70 or more years younger than them.

> *"I like younger women. Their stories are shorter."*
> - Tom McGuane

Even the self-help industry has started to specialize in age-difference relationships. In 1990, Sandra Reishus of Sacramento, CA founded YMOW (Younger Men, Older Women), a singles dating service which specializes in finding dating partners for women who prefer younger men. She is also writing a book on this topic. Men wanting to date women in their early twenties can get the book *"How to Date Younger Women, For Men Over 35"* by R. Don Steele.

At the time of my writing this book, a 22-year-old female friend is marrying a 47-year-old man. Another friend of mine, now 32, told me her best relationship was when she was 19 and went out with a 39-year-old man; the relationship lasted five years. The point is that the age difference factor is up to you and your partner, and no one else. There are more problems as the age difference becomes greater, but many relationships with unbelievable differences have worked for substantial periods. It will also depend on whether you consider the length of the relationship as the determining factor for its success. Because marriages have lasted many years, they haven't necessarily been happy ones.

Likes Attract - Sometimes

> *"Love is blind but marriage is a real eye opener."*
>
> *- Unknown Wise Person*

Most sociologists and anthropologists conclude that we tend to be attracted to people like ourselves - those from the same socioeconomic class, with similar levels of education, with similar physical characteristics, and with the same ethnic background. Their belief is that we will reap the most rewards from meeting people who have the same values as us, both in personal and business life. Many of the singles advertisements represent men and women looking for dating partners with the same interests.

The notion that a couple should have the same interests is somewhat limiting. Undoubtedly, the most interesting woman I have ever had a serious relationship with was the most different from me. When we first met, I thought that she was too intellectual and cultured for my taste. Our interests had little in common. I rushed through our first coffee date - to get it over with as soon as possible - thinking that I wouldn't date her again. However, a few days later, I phoned her when I was searching for a tennis partner. After a few more encounters, I fell in love with a charming, intellectual, athletic, attractive, and independent woman. I learned many things from her and she learned many things from me. In retrospect, this was the most exciting relationship I have ever had.

Some sociologists are of the persuasion that compatibility shouldn't depend so much on having the same interests as on having the same values. Different interests can actually add to compatibility. Liberals can form meaningful, and happy relationships with conservatives. Creative, unstructured men can be happy with structured, meticulous women. Many happy couples have little in common.

Your Singles Advantage

- **You don't have to explain why you are out late**
- **You can talk to yourself for hours**
- **Silence is golden**

Placing too much emphasis on compatibility based on common interests and similar goals is limiting. Two people in a relationship can develop new interests by sharing those which they don't have in common. The ability to communicate and mutual respect are just as, and possibly more, important than common interests. More than similar interests, the issue of similar core beliefs and compatible values (i.e. honesty and lifestyle choices) should determine if two people are right for each other. What matters most is whether the two people are connected morally and spiritually.

When you are searching for a dating partner, a person with a sense of humor should be high on your list. A study by Connecticut College psychologist Bernard Murstein found that humor is indicative of values, interests, intelligence, imagination, and needs. You will likely need a great sense of humor yourself, if you want to become attached to someone with one. Murstein found that men and women with similar senses of humor are more likely to love each other and want to marry. Once they marry, they also stay together longer. In exceptional relationships, love and laughter go hand in hand.

Is It Love Or A Fatal Attraction?

Love is magical and there are many forms of love. One state can be too magical; it can end up being a fatal attraction. Freud said that love is a state of temporary psychosis. Undoubtedly, he was referring to the obsessive and dangerous state of infatuation.

Infatuation normally is the state of romantic love that one experiences with a person whom one hasn't known a long time, and doesn't know intimately. People usually get infatuated with a somewhat mysterious individual who is hard to get. The person is either married, wooed by many others, or lives in a foreign country. The chase provides some of the excitement. Infatuation is an obsessive state of love, which hits all age groups, but is more suited for teenagers than for older adults. "Attachment junkies" of all ages are likely to get regularly stricken by infatuation; this leads them into short, rocky love affairs.

> *"Love is a grave mental illness."*
>
> *- Plato*

Infatuated individuals experience emotional highs and lows ranging from euphoria to despair. "Love at first sight" can be dangerous; it rarely leads to marriage, or a lifelong intimate relationship. Infatuation is often solely based on either physical beauty, charisma, youth, fame, wealth, or material possessions.

Freud was right about certain states of romantic love representing a state of temporary psychosis. When infatuation hits us, emotion and logic can go flying out the window, at least temporarily. Uncontrolled emotions lead us to overlook the negative traits in the individual. This results in an unhealthy and unworkable relationship. After failure hits, our intellect returns, and we end up wondering what we saw in the person in the first place.

Would You Choose Sex Or A Home Cooked Meal?

The sex drive can add to the dating dilemma. To some people, sex is no big deal. In a survey cited in *Homemaker's* magazine, 20 percent of the people surveyed said they would choose to eat a home-cooked meal over the opportunity to have sex. Personally, my choice would depend on how long it has been since I last ate. Recall the connection that researchers found between being physically fit and being able to perform sexually. Physically fit individuals report greater sexual frequency and more satisfying sex. It could be that most of the people who would choose the home-cooked meal are people who are already overweight and physically out of shape.

> *"It doesn't matter what you do in the bedroom as long as you don't do it in the street and frighten the horses."*
>
> *- Mrs. Patrick Campbell (British Actress)*

150

Many other singles are very interested in sex; some are even obsessed about it. A recent survey revealed that 54 percent of men and 19 percent of women say they think about sex daily. To help men and women in their sexual adventures, a variety of books have been written about the subject including such fascinating titles as *"How To Have Sex In Public Without Being Noticed"* and *"101 Things Not To Say During Sex."*

For many physically fit singles, who would choose sex over a home cooked meal, a common problem is a lack of opportunity, instead of a lack of interest, or a lack of energy and ability. Raw lust - provided there is some opportunity - is the only thing needed to drive them to action. Psychologists say recreational sex, especially by people going for records, is practiced by insecure individuals trying to prove their sexuality. You may feel that sexual satisfaction is a hat trick with three different partners all in one night. Alternatively, a one-night stand with one partner where you can make a quick get-a-way may appeal to you. However, on this subject I shall remain agnostic. I will leave the choice up to you. Who am I to say whether you truly enjoy this? Nonetheless, for most people, sex is significantly more satisfying when there is an emotional attachment to the other person.

"You act like the type of man who is into one-night stands."

"Not me. One-night stands are much too long for me!"

At times, sexual attraction leads to intimate relationships, and even marriage; however, a relationship based purely on physical attraction normally doesn't last. Many beautiful women and handsome men, who hypnotize members of the opposite sex with their physical features, are dumped by their partners shortly after the romance commences, simply because the whole basis for the relationship was physical attraction. Sex can in itself become routine and boring if the relationship has no other foundation.

151

Inside The Singles-Club Asylum

Your Singles Advantage

- **You don't have to falsely claim that you aren't married**
- **You can have three dates in one day**

A few years ago, I found myself spending a Friday night in a San Francisco nightclub with a woman from Georgia named Elaine. As we chatted, I kept noticing how almost everyone in the place was running an act about who they were. Everyone was trying to be like everyone else - with no one really knowing who they were supposed to be. Frankly speaking, almost everyone in the place was phonier than a tree full of elephants. This Halloween scene of paste-on smiles and masks of false happiness was starting to get to me when Elaine suggested that we leave. She must have had the same thoughts as mine, because she said something like: "Ernie, it is a good thing that we came here tonight. This bizarre scene confirms why I don't go to these places more than once every two years or so."

The meat market of the singles bar is okay if you like going to the circus. However, the chances of meeting someone genuine inside the singles-club asylum is slim indeed. People meet and get to know each other's genuine selves best when they are sharing activities over a few meetings. The problem with the singles bar scene is that everyone is acting out some character they would like to be, or some character they feel is more appealing to people than the real them. If someone with a false act appeals to you, the real person will be a disappointment when you get to know the person better. You will have been sold a false bill of goods; you certainly won't like someone who is trying to be someone other than who she or he is.

A disadvantage of singles bars and dances is the pressure on people to make contact and impress quickly with their wit and artificial charm. People are good actors; they aren't their true selves in these places. The result is a mismatch of values and interests which shows up if two people meet again in a less superficial atmosphere. The majority of successful singles conclude that the best way to meet people is by participating in activities which they genuinely enjoy. In this way, they don't end up wasting time if they don't meet someone on any particular day.

> *"If you want to catch a trout, don't fish in a herring barrel."*
>
> *- Ann Landers on singles bars*

Note that I am not ruling out singles clubs. Some cohabiting couples have met in bars. The point is that the majority of people don't. Couples outside Western societies rarely, if ever, meet in bars. In Western societies, bars and other singles joints are favorite meeting places with a low success rate for developing relationships.

Meeting By Other Than Chance

If your life is complete in terms of career and leisure pursuits, but not in companionship with the opposite sex, where do you go to look for a potential partner? There are millions of singles out there searching for love. If you find random meetings with strangers unnerving, you don't have to give up the hunt. You can always engage one or more of the many electronic courtship services now available. These include photo, video, and computer dating as well as singles advertisements in various newspapers and magazines.

Dating services are constantly evolving. In early 1995, *The European* magazine reported that the associates of Grace Bridal of Yokohama started offering the first Internet marriage service to Japanese singles. These on-line marriage specialists find singles a suitable partner, but they don't just stop there. They will also check his or her history, financial status, astrological sign, and vital statistics.

> *"Computer dating? It's terrific if you're a computer!"*
>
> *- Rita Mae Brown*

Many singles aren't willing to leave their love lives subject to chance. Instead of letting fate bring Mr. Right or Ms. Right, these singles are using dating services which are supposed to be more scientific in bringing the "right" dating partner to them. Dating services used to have much more stigma years ago than they have today. People using dating services cite the following advantages:

* People are there for the same reason - to meet someone.
* With people working longer hours, they have less opportunity to meet others after work.

* With more people working at home, many people don't have a chance to meet someone at work.
* With urbanization and no sense of community, many mobile people have to look elsewhere to meet others.

It is important to be careful with dating services. Many make unrealistic promises and claims which they aren't able to keep. Besides being extremely disappointed, you could wind up with a lot less money in your bank account than you started with.

> *"She deserves a good husband. Marry her before she finds one."*
>
> *- Oscar Levant*

It is much more acceptable to use the singles ads for connecting with potential partners today than it was five or ten years ago. All kinds of people now use these with varying degrees of success. Career people including doctors, lawyers, and engineers, who are too busy with their work and have little time for traditional dating, find the singles ads an effective way to meet new people. Just reading the ads can be interesting; some ads can be most intriguing. For example, the following one in the *Globe & Mail* caught my attention.

> *Admirers in the conventional sense I have in abundance, and they disinterest me. Stunning, young, assertive, independent, unattainable. Based in London, travels worldwide. Completely in love with my special interest. Seeks male devotee. Essential you're in a powerful position with control over others. Adds to my amusement. Behind closed doors I snap my fingers. My whims. My games. My rules. Our rules. Our secret.*
>
> *- Box 2862, The Globe & Mail*

You are probably thinking: "Ernie, so what happened when you responded?" Actually, even if I was interested, I wouldn't have responded because singles advertisements aren't to my taste. However, some people swear by them. Barbara Hammond of Bellingham, WA was divorced and looking to meet eligible men when she had a chance encounter with another woman. The woman was about to get married to a man she met after using the singles ads for over eighteen months. This woman's dating success got Barbara interested in using the singles ads, which she herself has now used successfully. Barbara has

> *"I know the difference between a good man and a bad one, but I haven't decided which I like better."*
>
> *- Mae West*

written a great book called *"Secrets of Meeting People Through The Personals"* for people who are interested in how to utilize the singles ads most effectively. I highly recommend this book if this mode of meeting others appeals to you.

Reasonable And Unreasonable Places To Connect

By now, you should realize that in order to meet people, you must increase your visibility. Nobody is going to come pounding at your door hoping to meet you. The more activities that you get immersed in, the more choice of people you will have, and the more chance you will have to meet someone special. Choose activities which you enjoy and don't make you feel out of place.

Again, in order that you increase your chances for meeting someone compatible, it is important for you to meet more people. You must be willing to take risks. Try to meet someone new on your unreasonable day. Do something unique, unreasonable, or totally silly. Also, be unreasonable in your choice of potential meeting places. I have found that places not normally rated the best meeting places are actually great places. These include libraries, grocery stores, and the post office.

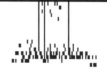

Your Singles Advantage

- **You can flirt with anyone, anytime, anywhere**
- **You can have a one-night stand without feeling guilty about cheating**

Here are some meeting places to consider, both reasonable and unreasonable:

- ♥ On cruise lines
- ♥ At dancing classes
- ♥ At church
- ♥ While walking your dog
- ♥ Weddings
- ♥ Spectator's sports events
- ♥ At computer or music stores
- ♥ Art galleries, museums, and the opera
- ♥ At the food market

- ♥ Libraries
- ♥ Airports
- ♥ Shopping malls
- ♥ At tennis, golf, badminton
- ♥ Political rallies
- ♥ Join a bridge club
- ♥ Singles clubs
- ♥ At other people's parties
- ♥ Coffee bars
- ♥ Throw a party (Don't forget to invite me; I like parties.)
- ♥ Non-profit organizations where you volunteer
- ♥ On an airplane
- ♥ Business and professional conferences
- ♥ College night courses
- ♥ Gourmet club

Patience is important when you are meeting others. Choosing surroundings, where there is no need to rush, and no pressure on you to impress, will increase your chances to meet someone you find interesting. Studies show that almost 75 percent of meaningful relationships are initiated where there is little pressure or intention to meet a partner. Activities or events, which allow people to meet on several occasions, are most conducive for intimate relationships to develop. Locations, where people are learning and sharing their points of view, are ripe for creating lasting relationships.

> *"You know you're in love when you don't want your girlfriend hanging around the joint you picked her up in."*
>
> *- From B.C. cartoon strip by Gart*

Get involved in activities, such as playing tennis at a club, where there is a good deal of social interaction. You will get to know people better when you meet them through a common interest or cause. More time is available to help you decide whether you should proceed further with that person. There isn't as much pressure as with nightclubs, singles ads, or dating services. Being relaxed and sincere is important. When people are actively engaged in many social activities which involve meeting others, opportunities for meeting someone interesting and compatible seem to arise. Paradoxically, when people aren't desperately seeking a dating partner, they often end up meeting someone interesting.

10. Flying Solo To Greater Heights

Look Inside If You Want To Find More Outside

The premise of this book is all unattached individuals can make their lives worthwhile and satisfying by enjoying the many pleasures that the single lifestyle offers. What singles require for success is an important mission or purpose, a sense of community based on a few close relationships, high self-esteem, and the ability to enjoy being alone. Much of this book has focused on the external world. We can achieve a certain degree of happiness in this world by reaching outward. Playing tennis, socializing with friends and acquaintances, traveling to exotic destinations, and going to the opera can give us a certain amount of pleasure in life. However, we must not forget the pleasures available to us when we cultivate our inner selves. The external world will offer only occasional and sporadic pleasures, if we haven't taken time to develop our spiritual selves. To get more out of the external world, we must tune into the inner world.

The spiritual self, probably the most important element for a rewarding life once our basic necessities have been satisfied, is usually the most neglected, ignored, or denied by people in our materialistically oriented society. Many singles are looking for something external to fill a void that can only be filled by developing a rich inner world. Society teaches us to value materialistic things and to ignore the intangible inner resources we all possess. The easy life is supposed to be just around the corner with the arrival of a new job, a big lottery win, or a new marriage partner. Desperate, externally-oriented singles want

> *"It is those of us who have a deep and real inner life who are best able to deal with the irritating details of outer life."*
>
> *- Evelyn Underhill*

157

marriage so badly that they often drive it away from themselves. As the years go by, singles living solely in the outer world find it more and more difficult to connect with other singles for a long-term relationship. They are looking for a savior as an outside source, when, in fact, the savior is an inside source. Outer-directed singles are at the mercy of parental and societal judgment which serves to limit opportunities for personal growth and development.

Taoism, like most religions, teaches us that when we look within ourselves, we find all that we need to make our lives happy and fulfilling. By searching within, we achieve clarity; life becomes effortless because we gain simplicity. Taoism stresses that simplicity is the ultimate expression of personal power. The inner world is the foundation for self-confidence and self-worth.

Internal orientation may not sound important to individuals in their teens or early twenties, but this is an essential ingredient for self-development as we grow older. The spiritual self is attained through much higher levels of consciousness than those used in sports, entertainment, or working. Well-balanced singles aren't at the mercy of the external world, because they have taken the time to develop a rich internal world.

The inner world holds the key to life filled with joy, satisfaction, and happiness. Committing yourself to the inner life, and the voice within, will result in strength and confidence not available in the outer world. The way to escape loneliness and despair is to develop your spirituality. Self-development can be mysterious, but it is also wondrous and fascinating. Self-questioning and personal growth result in self-determination which brings greater freedom. You must look inside, if you want to find more outside.

For Those Patient Enough To Wait For A Soulmate

"The best love affairs are those we never had."

- Norman Lindsay

Only by developing your spiritual world can you fly solo to greater heights. Because like tends to attract like, having developed an inner world may help you attract someone with the same higher consciousness. If you are tuned into your inner world, you will have a certain mystique to others because you have inner peace and a daily purpose. Other in-tune singles will recognize these intangible qualities in you. They will be attracted to you, because they feel comfortable with someone who doesn't grasp, smother, or cling to them.

"Distrust all those who love you extremely upon a very slight acquaintance and without viable reason."

- Lord Chesterfield

Many optimistic singles believe in soulmate relationships based on similar levels of higher consciousness. These relationships offer more opportunity than the normal relationships prevalent in Western societies. Soulmate relationships aren't based on superficial, external characteristics, such as social class, income levels, education, race, or religion. The underlying characteristics for soulmate relationships are common inner values of kindness, decency, sincerity, integrity, and courage. Soulmates want the same things out of life and are on similar levels of personal growth and consciousness.

Two friends of mine, Howard and Debra, are in a true soulmate relationship. Six years after getting married, they are still as affectionate towards each other as they were when they started going out. I have never seen another relationship quite like this one, although I am sure there are thousands more like it. Why do a small number of couples wind up in these great relationships? I don't have an answer for this, as I don't have an answer for why only a minority of people find their ultimate purpose in life which they pursue with passion. Perhaps it depends on how much we are willing to sacrifice in time, effort, energy, commitment, and patience for creating these things for ourselves.

"Who longest waits most surely wins."

- Helen Hunt Jackson

"Experts" who write on soulmate relationships say that if your soulmate is to appear, he or she will appear when you are ready for a soulmate. Your level of consciousness and personal growth will determine when you are ready. You can't go desperately searching for a soulmate all around Seattle or Boston or New York. Self-improvement is a time for preparation and a prelude to meeting a soulmate. You must learn to be relaxed and enjoy life while you wait for your soulmate to arrive. However, you can't wait at home to be discovered. You must get yourself out of your apartment or house and spend time at those life-enhancing activities which contribute to your personal growth and increased consciousness.

Soulmate relationships are joyful, rewarding, and life-enhancing. However, these relationships aren't without their difficulties. Even with a true soulmate, feelings of fear associated with rejection, vulnerability, and intimacy may surface at the outset. A soulmate relationship isn't the perfect relationship with a perfect partner, although it offers a lot more than a less-than-satisfying compromise, or a relationship based mainly on external factors, such as having a lot of money, liking the same sports, or both partners being good dancers.

> *"No matter how qualified or deserving we are, we will never reach a better life until we can imagine it for ourselves and allow ourselves to have it."*
>
> *- From "One" by Richard Bach*

If you create a soulmate relationship, you will recognize it as one in which your partner represents possibilities instead of limitations. Finding the right partner or soulmate is dependent on your ability to develop a clear picture of your feelings and wants. With a soulmate, you don't give up your freedom; you gain even more freedom to live and grow.

What It Takes To Be A High-Flying Single

High-flying singles feel that it is better to wait for a soulmate who never comes, instead of having to settle for a dull or less-than-satisfying compromise. High-flying singles can afford to wait for a soulmate who may never come, because their single life is much more satisfying and rewarding than most marriages. They know how to enjoy life while waiting for their soulmate to arrive. Well-balanced singles know how to create happy, satisfying lifestyles for themselves. If Mr. Right or Ms. Right shows up - that's great; if he or she doesn't show up - that's okay too! If their soulmate fails to arrive in this lifetime, it doesn't really matter, since they are already as happy, or happier, than most married people. High-flying singles are involved in personal growth. They are flying solo to greater heights, because they have developed, or are in the process of developing, the following important traits:

High-flying singles are different and don't mind standing out in a crowd. These well-balanced individuals don't spend their time trying to fit in with the rest of society. High-flying singles aren't approval seekers like most people. They have no problem being different. Whether at work or at play, they care little about what others think.

They don't let society dictate how they should behave, and they won't engage in small talk just because it is the polite thing to do.

To creative singles, conformity is dull and interferes with their ability to do the new and rewarding. Not being approval seekers, high-flying singles have more freedom and flexibility to pursue a lifestyle which contributes to personal growth and satisfaction. Because they don't mind being different, well-balanced singles don't follow the herd and fall for every new fad that comes along.

> *"It's better to be a lion for a day than a sheep all your life."*
>
> *- Sister Elizabeth Kenny*

High-flying singles have a great sense of humor which contributes to the magnetic and magical quality about them. Their sense of humor isn't something they were born with; it is a trait which they themselves developed. Their strong sense of humor is an important asset for getting through rough times, since it helps them cope with minor and major problems, as well as adversity. Their ability to laugh and enjoy the moment contributes to their ability to enjoy life to the fullest, and quickly overcome the emotional lows which tend to immobilize others.

High-flying singles can laugh at their problems. They don't always take themselves, others, or the world seriously. They can be silly and act dumb just for the heck of it. They realize how much a sense of humor in a prospective partner appeals to them. They know that their own sense of humor is a trait to which most other high-flying singles are attracted.

High-flying singles treasure solitude. They realize that the capacity to be alone is a valuable resource. Solitude is a time for reflection and self-discovery. High-flying singles, like many highly creative poets, philosophers, and artists, encounter peak experiences when they are alone. They may be alone, but they don't feel alone. The pleasures of solitude contribute to a natural high and can be a spiritual experience for them.

Some exceptional high-flying singles intentionally seek days or weeks of solitude for self-discovery. Being alone is time to get in touch with one's deepest inner feelings, and discover what one really wants, instead of what others may expect one to want. Time alone is also for sorting out one's ideas and changing one's attitude about life. High-flying singles are rarely lonely, because they are able to overcome loneliness whenever it strikes. Solitude is something they use to create and maintain a better world for themselves. High-flying singles will go to great lengths to preserve their privacy.

High-flying singles are highly independent and value their freedom. They are self-confident and know what is important to them. Although they can be deeply sensitive and loving in relationships, well-balanced singles are looking for a relationship which provides independence for both themselves and their partners. They realize that a relationship where both individuals have independence is superior to a relationship where one or both partners are highly dependent.

> *"No bird soars too high, if he soars with his own wings."*
>
> *- William Blake*

Needy and dependent singles find it hard to like or love high-flying singles because high-flying singles are adamant about their independence. High-flying singles refuse to be dependent on a partner, or be depended upon by a partner, because these relationships are exploitative and unhealthy. When someone starts clinging to a high-flying single, he or she will pull back emotionally, and may even disappear physically. You won't find high-flying singles trying to get involved in numerous love and friendship relationships. To them, quality is more important than quantity.

High-flying singles have a zest for life. These enthusiastic singles project a constant zest for living, and don't have to rely on outside influences to excite them. Well-balanced singles are capable of enjoying television, parties, night clubs, and taverns, but you won't find them spending too much time at any of these. Instead, you will find them enjoying more rewarding activities, ones which unenthusiastic singles miss out on.

High-flying singles know how to enjoy the moment. Since they realize that they may remain single for some time, they don't waste time wishing circumstances were different. Well-balanced singles don't expect a potential marriage partner to come along and solve all their problems. Because they savor the now, they don't waste much time regretting the past, or worrying about the future.

162

High-flying singles don't suffer from a victim mentality. A great mystery in life to high-flying singles is why so many people would rather blame the world, and so few people are willing to take responsibility for their actions. High-flying singles know about the dangers of the victim mentality. They know that people with a victim mentality will never be liberated. People with a victim mentality will always set it up so that they are victims to satisfy their perverted belief systems.

Your Singles Advantage

- **You don't have to report to anyone before you go out**
- **You can go on a vacation where you want to go**

High-flying singles are truly liberated people because they know there is discrimination of all kinds, as well as many other roadblocks; however, they have decided to make their lives work by using their creativity. High-flying singles know that liberation takes effort and persistence - not someone else's, but their own. They have a positive attitude about life. They invest their energy in creating opportunity for adventure, community, and satisfaction. Happiness is a choice and not something beyond their control.

High-flying singles know how to deal with failure and rejection. Unlike the majority in society, high-flying singles know how to fail. To well-balanced singles, failure is a means to success. They realize that the best way to double their success rate is to double their failure rate. To be successful in love and life, they may have to experience many setbacks. Only by having experienced regular failure will they have achieved regular success.

Well-balanced singles are able to take rejection by others. When these healthy singles find someone who is valuable and precious to them, they go out of their way to let the individual know. When in the company of other people, they can experience a wide range of emotions including joy, affection, frustration, pain, confusion, self-respect, and even anger. They aren't ashamed to show these emotions.

High-flying singles are adventurous. They like to explore the world around them. They like to travel to new destinations, to meet new people, and to discover new things. Being moderate risk takers, they will try activities with an element of danger. Naturally curious and not threatened by the unknown, high-flying singles want to learn every present moment of their lives. Because they seek out experiences that are new and unfamiliar to them, they have unlimited opportunities for doing, thinking, feeling, loving, laughing, and living.

Flying Solo To Heights That Others Haven't Dreamed About

"Zelinski's books have motivated me to quit my good job, give up a decent marriage, and become so different that even my mother doesn't like me. I am now the ultimate successful failure."

I have found that some people embrace my books for all the wrong reasons; I trust that you won't do the same. Thomas Carlyle (1795-1881) said: "The best effect of any book is that it excites the reader to self-activity." I hope that this book will have opened a new way of life for you. Now is the time to take all the important material that is relevant to your life and "run with it." Hopefully, you will be motivated in some way to undertake some of the difficult things in the short term, so that your life becomes easier in the long term. As you have learned by now, being single in a couple-crazed world isn't easy. However, by following the principles of this book, it isn't that difficult to create a rewarding life while you are unattached.

Experiencing the joy of being single is an attitude about life. Remember that marriage is not a panacea for loneliness and dejection. The cure for loneliness and dejection is to learn how to be happy as a single. No marriage partner can guarantee happiness for you. You don't need another person to make you whole and give you meaning. Instead of generating reasons why you can't make it alone, create reasons why you can.

Being single isn't better or worse than marriage or couplehood.

Singlehood is different in experience and tone. It has its unique challenges and opportunities as does couplehood. Being single allows you to experience life in a unique way, much different from life experienced by someone who is attached.

Wanting a marriage partner to make you feel happy, satisfied, secure, and whole is looking to the outside for someone to satisfy needs that only you can satisfy internally. Losing contact with the higher self can result in despair and depression in your mature years. You are ultimately responsible for your emotions, actions, purpose, and financial state in life. The way out of loneliness, rejection, and dejection is to tune into the inner world. Taking responsibility for developing your spiritual self will go a long way to creating those conditions necessary for a satisfying and happy life.

> *"Learn to enjoy the little things in life because the big ones don't come around very often."*
>
> *- Andy Rooney*

If you are like most singles, you have the luxury of plenty of leisure time to do things by yourself, as well as with others. The quality of your life will depend on how you utilize that leisure time. Being your own person means that you get to choose how you utilize your leisure time so that it reflects your individuality and personality. You get to choose your own schedule without having to compromise for someone else's likes and dislikes. Using your leisure time wisely ensures that you will keep growing and learning as you venture through the different phases of life. In your quest for love and purpose, don't forget about life's simple pleasures. If you're feeling bored or lonely, then:

* Visit the local coffee bar and watch the people
* Have a heart-to-heart conversation with a six-year-old
* Go for a two-hour walk in the park
* Take a nap
* Do something unreasonable
* Plan a party and invite many interesting people
* Walk barefoot through a stream
* Read Jane Austen or Danielle Steele down by the river
* Attend a concert
* Take up a new sport just for the fun of it
* Look at the beauty of nature all around you

* Treat yourself to a mini-vacation
* Start writing your book
* Spend the entire day in a park just watching people
* Watch children and pets at play
* Phone an old friend whom you haven't talked to for awhile

> *"All times are beautiful for those who maintain joy within themselves; but there is no happy or favorable time for those with disconsolate or orphaned souls."*
>
> *- Rosalia Castro*

Be sure to seek out new people, new places, and new points of view. The unknown and unexpected will add to your experience of life. Activities such as music, gardening, meditating, and taking a walk in the park can be spiritual in nature. Risk, experiment, and don't forget to have some fun while you are at it. Generate the creative energy to continue in a positive manner, regardless of which negative events seem to conspire against you. Find reasons to do the important things, instead of not to do them.

Making it alone requires that you have some major purpose in life - something which motivates you to get up a half-hour before your alarm goes off in the morning. Seek a career or job where you can make money doing what you enjoy. Creative employment, where you get to express yourself and work for some higher purpose in life, will go a long way towards making life worth living - with or without a partner.

It is also important to establish some close, meaningful relationships. Few people can be loners and still be happy. Connections to special friends, relatives, and acquaintances are necessary for a sense of community. Love from others at some level is necessary to feel appreciated.

> *"Whatever with the past has gone, the best is always yet to come."*
>
> *- Lucy Larcom*

If you want to meet someone special to marry, or create that soulmate relationship, do whatever is necessary to make it happen. Don't wait at home to be discovered. Make yourself available to others and you are closer to attracting the soulmate whom you are patiently waiting for. Remember to do everything you can to experience the joys of life while you patiently wait for your soulmate.

166

One of the biggest advantages of being single is the many interests and relationships you can develop as sources of stimulation. While you patiently wait for a soulmate or dating partner to appear in your life, you can enjoy a lifestyle which is enhanced by a satisfying career and personal leisure achievements. This is an opportunity to make choices and live for your goals and dreams.

Remember what a luxury singlehood is. You have the freedom many don't. You can choose when you want to be alone and when you want to be with others. Don't spend your time dreaming and fantasizing about how much better things would be if only you were in a relationship, made more money, or had a better job. The importance of living the moment should be as clear to you as a Zen master's moment of truth. If you postpone the chance to live life, it may slip away altogether. The time to start living is now.

Being single allows you the luxury of doing what you want, when you want, with whomever you want. You get to celebrate your individuality and come to terms with who you really are, and not what someone else wants you to be. Freedom is your treasure; you get to determine the quality of your life. Singlehood is an opportune time to discover for yourself that you are more of an individual than society says you are supposed to be. Realizing your higher self will make you a much more creative and dynamic individual. Your life will be a joy to behold, because it has richness and quality.

Again, being single isn't easy. Half the battle is getting your attitude in shape, and focusing your energy in such a way as to enjoy the people and events that enhance your life. The purpose of life is to live. Self-fulfillment depends on attitude, courage, patience, perseverance, and focused effort. With these assets - especially attitude and sustained effort - being single isn't that difficult.

> *"Is not life a hundred times too short for us to bore ourselves?"*
>
> *- Friedrich Nietzsche*

The golden rule for living a satisfying singles lifestyle is that you like and enjoy yourself. You must be loyal to yourself - treat yourself like you would your best friend or ideal lover. Above all, have a love affair with yourself. Remember that before you can truly make it with someone else, you must make it with yourself. As a high-flying single, you are free as a bird to fly solo to heights most attached people have never dreamed of reaching.

If you have enjoyed this book and have any thoughts, comments, or experiences that you would like to share with me, I will be happy to hear from you. Address all letters to:

Ernie Zelinski
c/o Visions International Publishing
P.O. Box 4072
Edmonton, Alberta
Canada, T6E 4S8

Bibliography And Recommended Reading

L. Barbara Hammond's *Secrets Of Meeting People Through The Personals* (Starr Publishing, 1994)

Helen Fisher's *Anatomy Of Love - The Mysteries of Mating, Marriage, And Why We Stray* (Ballantine Books, 1992)

Michele Weiner-Davis's *Fire Your Shrink* (Simon & Schuster, 1995)

Michele Weiner-Davis's *Divorce Busting* (Simon & Schuster, 1992)

Dr. David Weeks's and Jamie James's *Eccentrics* (Weidenfeld and Nicolson Publishers, Britain, 1995)

Thomas Moore's *Soul Mates - Honoring the Mysteries of Love and Relationships* (HarperCollins, 1994)

Susan Rabin's *How To Attract Anyone, Anytime, Anyplace - The Smart Guide To Flirting* (Penguin Books, 1993)

Michael Broder's *The Art Of Living Single* (Avon Books, 1990)

Susan Page's *If I'm So Wonderful, Why Am I Still Single?* (Bantam, 1988)

David Wallechinsky's and Amy Wallace's *The Book Of Lists - The '90s Edition* (Little Brown & Company, 1993)

Richard Bach's *Illusions: The Adventures Of A Reluctant Messiah* (Dell, 1977)

Richard Bach's *Bridge Across Forever* (William Morrow & Company, Inc., 1984)

Richard Bach's *One* (William Morrow & Company, Inc., 1988)

Shakti Gwain's *Living In The Light* (Whatever Publishing, 1986)

Antoine de Saint Exupery's *The Little Prince* (Harcourt, Brace, Jovanocich, Inc., 1943)

Appendix - The Easy Rule Of Life

DO: **THE EASY AND COMFORTABLE**	DO: **THE DIFFICULT AND UNCOMFORTABLE**
⬇	⬇
LIFE ENDS UP BEING: **DIFFICULT**	**LIFE ENDS UP BEING:** **EASY**

"The Easy Rule Of Life" teaches us that when we take the easy and comfortable route, life turns out to be difficult. Ninety percent of us choose this route because short-term comfort appeals to us. The other option available to us is to take the difficult and uncomfortable route. When we do this, life is easy. People who take this route know that they must experience occasional short-term discomfort for long-term gains.

The Easy Rule Of Life applies to practically all areas of our lives. For example, if you want to be healthy and in great physical condition, you must exercise regularly and vigorously. This is somewhat difficult and uncomfortable. If you choose the easy route instead by watching TV, you will be out of shape and wind up unhealthy. Your self-esteem will also suffer. Life will end up being difficult! Here is another example involving teenagers: After reading about The Easy Rule Of Life in *"The Joy Of Not Working,"* New York resident Lynne Tillotson in a letter written to me stated:

> *"I teach Juvenile Delinquents in a NYS Division for Youth Facility .... I made copies of The Easy Rule Of Life. The kids were interested and enthused and came up with parallels in their own lives that amazed me. e.g. Easy money selling drugs leads to family pain, danger, death, jail, etc. If I had tried to bring these things up, it would have been preachy."*

The problem with choosing the comfortable way is that in the long run life becomes difficult. The biggest obstacle to success in life is the fear of the discomfort in doing the necessary things that we must do to attain success. We opt for the easy way because we are seeking comfort at all costs, but roads on which there is lots of traffic tend to have a lot of ruts. Choosing the easy way in life ensures that we wind up in one or more of these ruts - and the only difference between a rut and a grave are the dimensions! If you want success in life, you must do the difficult things at times. When you become successful in completing your important projects, your life will be easy and comfortable.

Resources - Publications

Childless By Choice
Subscriptions: $15 per year
Carin Smith, Editor, Phone (509) 763-2112
PO Box 695, Leaenworth, WA, 98826

Single Again - (The Magazine For The Divorced, Separated or Widowed)
Subscriptions: $15 per year, $21 in Canada
Phone (510) 793-6315)
Len Harris, Executive Publisher
PO Box 1402, Union City, CA, 94587

Single Styles - (The Art of Single Living)
Subscriptions: $15 per year, $21 in Canada
Phone (813) 595-5008
PO Box 1257, Largo, FL, 34649-1257

Barbara Brabec's Self-Employment Survival Letter
(Bimonthly, $29 per year, $33 foreign in US Funds)
Barbara Brabec, Editor & Publisher, Ph. (708) 717-4188
P.O. Box 2127, Naperville, IL, 60567

The Newsletter of the Society for the Reduction of Human Labor
($25 per year)
Benjamin K. Hunnicutt, Coeditor
1610 E. College St., Iowa City, IA, 52245

Resources - Support Groups

Couch Potatoes (TV addict support group)
Contact: Robert Armstrong, Edler #2
PO Box 249, Dixon, CA, 95620

The Single Parent
Parents Without Partners, Inc.
Allan N. Glennon, Editor of magazine
8807 Colesville Rd., Silver Springs, MD, 20910

Single Parent Resource Center
Contact: Suzanne Jones, Executive Director
1165 Broadway, Rm 504, New York, NY, 10001

Resources - Support Groups (Continued)

National Workaholics Anonymous
PO Box 661501
Los Angeles, CA, 90066

Sexaholics Anonymous
(Offer a 12-step program for people seeking "sexual sobriety")
PO Box 300
Simi Valley, CA, 93062

Younger Men, Older Women
Sandre Reishus, Director & Founder
Phone (916) 452-3231
1403 28th St, Suite 206
Sacramento, CA, 95816

Resources - Interesting And Offbeat Organizations

The Boring Institute
Contact: Alan Caruba, Head and Expert in Boredom
Box 40
Maplewood, NJ, 07040

Institute of Totally Useless Skills
Contact: Rick Davis, Master of Uselessness
Phone (603) 654-5875
20 Richmond St., Dover, NH, 03820

International Organization of Nerds
Contact: Bruce L. Chapman, Supreme Archnerd
PO Box 118555, Cincinnati, OH, 45211

National Society for Prevention of Cruelty to Mushrooms
Contact: Brad Brown, President
1077 S. Airport Rd. W, Traverse City, MI, 49684

Benevolent and Loyal Order of Pessimists
Slogan: "In front of every silver lining, there's a dark cloud."
Contact: Jack Duvall, President
PO Box 1945, Iowa City, IA, 52244

The Joy Of Not Knowing It All

Profiting From Creativity At Work Or Play

Whether you are an artist, poet, or entrepreneur, this entertaining book is designed to help you profit from creativity at work and play. In a highly competitive and rapidly changing world, *The Joy Of Not Knowing It All* offers hope and opportunity. Ernie Zelinski inspires you to risk, be different, challenge the status quo, ruffle a few feathers, and in the process, truly make a big difference in this world.

This outstanding resource will help enhance the business performance of your staff and clients. Special prices apply for all individuals and organizations purchasing 10 or more copies.

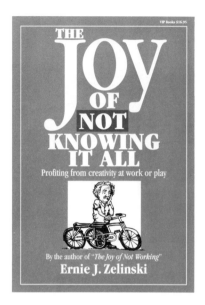

To order single copies on your credit card by telephone:

Call toll free 1-800-661-3649 in Canada and 1-800-356-9315 in the U.S.

In the U.S., to order <u>autographed</u> copies of *The Joy Of Not Knowing It All* by mail, send $19.95 per book (includes postage and handling).

In Canada, send $21.35 per book (includes $1.40 for GST).

Visions International Publishing   Ph. (403) 436-1798
P.O. Box 4072
Edmonton, Alberta
Canada, T6E 4S8

Make checks payable to Visions International Publishing

Name _____

Street_____

City _____ Province/State _____

Zip Or Postal Code _____

The Joy Of Not Being Married

The Essential Guide For Singles And Those Who Wish They Were

The Joy Of Not Being Married gives singles the essentials for living a happy and satisfying lifestyle filled with opportunities not available to married people. A fulfilling life is possible for all singles regardless of their sex, age, or past marital status.

Being happy being single requires that you get in touch with your interests, goals, and spirituality. *The Joy Of Not Being Married* shows you how to live life to the fullest by being happy with the most important person in your life - you.

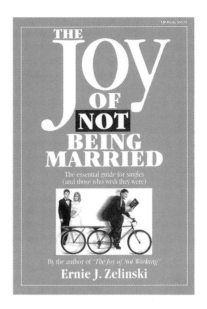

To order single copies on your credit card by telephone:

Call toll free 1-800-661-3649 in Canada and 1-800-356-9315 in the U.S.

In the U.S., to order <u>autographed</u> copies of *The Joy Of Not Being Married* by mail, send $19.95 per book (includes postage and handling).

In Canada, send $21.35 per book (includes $1.40 for GST).

Visions International Publishing   Ph. (403) 436-1798
P.O. Box 4072
Edmonton, Alberta
Canada, T6E 4S8

Make checks payable to Visions International Publishing

Name _____

Street_____

City _____ Province/State _____

Zip Or Postal Code _____

The Joy Of Not Working

A Book For The Retired, Unemployed, and Overworked

Ellen Roseman of *The Globe And Mail* in an article about *The Joy Of Not Working* suggested: "Give this book to someone who has just retired or been laid off."

By using practical examples, numerous illustrations, and entertaining exercises, Ernie Zelinski has written a bestselling book which is humorous and easy to read, but presents a serious and highly beneficial message on how to enjoy leisure like never before. Career practitioners, outplacement consultants, and health counselors are recommending this book in lifestyle courses.

To order single copies on your credit card by telephone:

Call toll free 1-800-661-3649 in Canada and 1-800-356-9315 in the U.S.

In the U.S., to order <u>autographed</u> copies of *The Joy Of Not Working* by mail, send $19.95 per book (includes postage and handling).

In Canada, send $21.35 per book (includes $1.40 for GST).

Visions International Publishing   Ph. (403) 436-1798
P.O. Box 4072
Edmonton, Alberta
Canada, T6E 4S8

Make checks payable to Visions International Publishing

Name _____

Street_____

City _____ Province/State _____

Zip Or Postal Code _____

About The Author

Ernie Zelinski is the author of the bestselling book *"The Joy Of Not Working"* which has sold over 50,000 copies in its English version and was recently published in both Chinese and Japanese. Feature articles about Ernie and *"The Joy Of Not Working"* have appeared in the Washington Post, Vancouver Sun, Oakland Tribune, Boston Herald, Seattle Post-Intelligencer, Toronto Star, and Globe and Mail. Ernie has also been interviewed on CBC TV's Venture, CTV's Dini Petty Show, and over 50 radio stations in the U.S. and Canada.

Ernie Zelinski

Ernie is also the author of *"The Joy Of Not Knowing It All"*, a bestselling book on creativity. As a professional speaker, Ernie has spoken on how to apply creativity to both business and leisure at many conferences and management retreats hosted by organizations such as BC Hydro, Canadian Association of Insurance Women, Certified General Accountants of BC, and Canadian Homecare Association. You can book Ernie for a conference keynote speech or company seminar by calling the following speaker bureau:

Linda Davidson
Can*Speak Presentations
Vancouver, BC
Phone (604) 986-6887 or (800) 665-7376

Ernie has an Engineering degree and a Master's in Business Administration. As a part-time instructor in business, he has taught his principles of creativity to students at the University of Alberta in Edmonton and Simon Fraser University and City University in Vancouver.

Ernie lives in Edmonton and spends as much time as he can in Vancouver, which he considers his second home. He has been 35 years old for the last several years, because he likes the age 35. Following his own advice, Ernie is a connoisseur of leisure and tries to maintain a four-hour work day for four days a week. Besides just hanging around his favorite coffee bars, Ernie enjoys cycling, tennis, reading, and traveling. Ernie is single, has never been married, and is patiently waiting for his soulmate to make her appearance.